ENAMOURED OF AN ASS

To Gill & Colin Graham-Stewart, who
also love donkeys
With all good wishes
from
Stella A. Walker.

'The Wild Asses Quench their Thirst' by Charles Henry Augustus Lutyens, 1829–1915

ENAMOURED OF AN ASS

A Donkey Anthology

Compiled by Stella Walker

With illustrations by Michael Lyne

ANGUS & ROBERTSON · PUBLISHERS

ANGUS & ROBERTSON . PUBLISHERS
London . Sydney . Melbourne . Singapore . Manila

First published by Angus and Robertson (UK) Ltd, 2, Fisher Street, London, WC1, in 1977

ISBN 0 207 95688 X

Printed in Great Britain by
Hazell Watson & Viney Ltd,
Aylesbury, Bucks

Designed by Peggy and
Drummond Chapman

CONTENTS

Other books by Stella A. Walker include:

Horses of Renown
The Controversial Horse
(*with R. S. Summerhays*)
Sporting Art: England 1700-1900

Anthologies:
Long Live The Horse!
In Praise of Horses
In Praise of Spring
In Praise of Kent

Editor of:
Summerhays Encyclopedia for Horsemen
(*sixth edition*)

FOREWORD

Over ninety years ago I first went riding on a donkey and I have been a lifelong admirer of the species ever since. In 1968 to my great pleasure I became President of the Donkey Show Society (later the Donkey Breed Society); two years later Stella Walker was appointed its second chairman. In this varied and well-chosen anthology she seems to capture the immense pleasure, interest and surprises the donkey has given to us both. Owners, admirers and even denigrators will all find it engrossing and delightful and I wish it every success.

R. S. Summerhays

Acknowledgements

The Compiler and Publishers have made every effort to trace the owners of copyright and apologize to any whom they have been unable to contact. They are indebted to the following for permission to reproduce published material:

Associated Book Publishers for an extract from *Winnie-the-Pooh* by A. A. Milne

Hugo Brunner for an extract from his article *Donkey Wheels as a Source of Power*

Cassell & Company Ltd. for an extract from *Brewer's Dictionary of Phrase and Fable*

Cassell & Company Ltd. for extracts from *People with Long Ears* by Robin Borwick

Centaur Press & M. R. de Wesselow for an extract from her book *Donkeys: Their Care and Management*

Constable & Company Ltd. for an extract from *Beasts and Saints* by Helen Waddell

Henry Cotton and the Donkey Breed Society Magazine for the article *Pacifico the Caddy*

Curtis Brown Ltd. for an extract from *My Kingdom for a Donkey* by Doris Rybot

C. N. de Courcy-Parry for his article *Dalesman's First Hunter*

Marjorie Dunkels for a poem from *Training Your Donkey*

'The Field' for articles by Tim Matthews and Stella Walker

Rumer Godden and Carmen Bernos de Gasztold for *The Prayer of the Donkey*

Victor Gollancz Ltd. for an extract from *Reminiscences of Affection* by Louis Untermeyer

Hamish Hamilton Ltd. for an extract from *South to Granada* by Gerald Brenan

George G. Harrap & Company Ltd. for two extracts from *Donkey* by Anthony Dent

Dorothy Hartley and 'The Guardian' for an article entitled *Donkey Work*

David Higham Associates Ltd. for an extract from *The Book of Beasts* by T. H. White published by Jonathan Cape

Hodder & Stoughton Ltd. for an extract from *The Man with the Donkey* by Sir Irving Benson

Hodder & Stoughton Ltd. for the poem *Donkey* by Bernard Spencer from a collection entitled *With Luck Lasting*

Dr. Stuart Hogg for the poem *Soliloquy*

Philip Howard and Times Newspapers Ltd. for an extract from an article in 'The Times'

Humphrey & Formula Press Pty. Ltd. for an extract from *Australian Donkeys* by Ann Walker

Hutchinson Publishing Group Ltd. for an extract from *Donkey Man* by Ron Brewer

Christopher Mathews & Times Newspapers Ltd. for his article *Wally on Margate Beach*

John Murray (Publishers) Ltd. for an extract from *The Wild Ass Free* by Michael Mason

'Nature' for an article by Frank C. Hibben

Penguin Books Ltd. for *Every Man to His Own Trade* and *One Master as Good as Another* from *Fables of Aesop* translated by S. A. Handford (Penguin Classics, New Edition 1964) pp. 115, 116. Copyright © S. A. Handford 1954

A. D. Peters & Company Ltd. for an article by Kenneth Allsop

Laurence Pollinger Ltd. and The Estate of the late Mrs. Frieda Lawrence for *The Ass* from *The Complete Poems of D. H. Lawrence* published by William Heinemann Ltd.

'Punch' for the poem *Donkey* by Gertrude Hind and for an article by E. V. Lucas entitled *You Ass*

Lady Swinfen for a personal letter published in *Donkeys Galore* (David & Charles)

The Literary Trustees of Walter De La Mare and The Society of Authors for *Nicholas Nye* from *The Collected Poems of Walter De La Mare*, 1969

Joan Wanklyn for the poem *Triptych*

Joan Warburg & The Mitre Press for the poems *Donkeys in Corfu* and *Dalmatian Donkeys*

Mrs. G. M. Watkins for *Prayer to Go to Paradise with the Donkeys* translated from the French of Francis Jammes by Vernon Watkins

A. P. Watt & Son, Mrs. D. E. Collins and J. M. Dent for *The Donkey* from *The Wild Knight* by G. K. Chesterton

A. P. Watt & Son, Mrs. George Bambridge & Eyre Methuen Ltd. for *Aboard the Ark* from *Legends of Evil* by Rudyard Kipling

The Baroness Wootton of Abinger and the Donkey Breed Society Magazine for her article *Francesca and Miranda*

Front of jacket illustration:
'Sheep And Donkeys On A Moor' by Thomas Sidney Cooper, 1803–1902, with grateful acknowledgement to the Cooling Gallery and the Medici Society.

Back of jacket illustration:
'Children Riding Donkeys On A Road' by Jacques Laurent Agasse, from the collection of Mr. and Mrs. Paul Mellon, Upperville, Virginia, U.S.A.

Grateful acknowledgements for the use of illustration are made to the following:

Australian Information Service	P. 183
Royal Academy of Arts	P. 180
British Museum	P. 157
Brighton Art Gallery	P. 101
Henry Cotton and the 'Daily Mail'	Pp. 74–75
Mrs. Margaret Care	P. 36
Courtauld Institute	Pp. 16–17, 81
Country Life	Pp. 43
Terence Cuneo and the Sladmore Gallery	P. 141
Anthony Dent	Pp. 8–9, 54, 106–107, 91
The Donkey Breed Society Magazine	Pp. 47, 93, 151
Joan Howard-Carter	P. 12
Irish Tourist Board,	contents page, P. 123
Mansell Collection	P. 177
Collection of Mr and Mrs Paul Mellon	P. 33
Norwich Union Insurance	Pp. 136–137
Radio Times Hulton Picture Library	Pp. 4, 29, 79, 116, 189
Sotheby & Co.	P. 161
Leesa Sandys Lumsdaine and the Tryon Gallery	P. 132
Tryon Gallery: Endpapers from a painting by John Emms, 1847–1912	
The Topkapi Palace Hazine Library	P. 55

The Compiler and Publishers are especially grateful to Mrs. Dorothy Morris who provided the photographs for pages 2, 27, 40–41, 59, 68–69, 70, 77, 147

For my grand-daughter,
Rebecca.

EXPLANATION

Titania: Methought I was enamoured of an ass
Midsummer Night's Dream

There have been many donkeys in my life since the first enchantment at the age of five by independent Neddy on Scarborough sands. I remember gentle Esmeralda, who, in spite of high hopes, never achieved maternity; and those desperate bicycle pursuits in the small hours after bold, unbiddable Bacchus, a Casanova wanderer leading in his wake ponies, hunters and Shires through a trail of broken fences. Very vividly I can recall the score of small Jamaican donkeys tied up every market day amid the heat and flies of a mountain village, girth-galled and overladen but sadly willing. And in Co. Kerry endearing Irish Sally and her shandrydan carrying churns every morning to the milk lorry with her furry brown foal gambolling alongside. Delinquents and delectables alike they won my heart.

Today when the donkey has become a V.I.P. and I am confronted in the show-ring by a long row of kind eyes, indicative ears and soft velvet muzzles, I wish red rosettes could be universal, for, you see, over the years I have become not just enamoured of an ass but besotted about all donkeys! That is the reason for this anthology.

S.A.W.

1. Donkeys Defined

DESIGNATION

DONKEY: an ass. The word is of comparatively recent origin, being first recorded about 1782 . . . and seems at first to have rhymed with "monkey". It is a diminutive and may be connected with "*dun*" in reference to its tint. "Dun" . . . was a familiar name for a horse, and the "donkey" is a smaller or more diminutive beast of burden.

Brewer's Dictionary of Phrase and Fable 1870

CUDDY

In the far north of England they call it a "cuddy". In north and east Yorkshire they prefer "fussock", while the alternative appellation "pronkus" is mostly confined to Lincolnshire. In Norfolk, Suffolk and north Essex they say "dicky"; in Hampshire, south-east Wiltshire and Dorset "nirrup". The variant synonyms "moke" and "neddy" are scattered widely around England, with a pocket of "mokus"-sayers in the south-west.

"Ass" is still the customary dialect word in about 20 districts spread across the country from Northumberland to west Sussex and from Norfolk to Staffordshire. But all these delicious ways of describing a grey quadruped with furry ears and a hee-haw are rapidly and inexorably being superseded by "donkey", a comparative newcomer to the language and a word of obscure, possibly slang, origin. The first recorded use of "donkey" was in 1785, and perhaps it infiltrated into standard English from Essex or Suffolk.

The oldest word for the creature is probably "ass", from the old English "assa", but it started to disappear when English began to be standardized after the Middle Ages, partly for reasons of politeness because its pronunciation became confused with that of "arse".

Philip Howard
The Times 1972

A harras of horses; a ragg of colts; a stud of mares; a pace of asses; a barren of mules.

Dame Julyana Berners
The Boke of St Albans c. 1388

Collecting peat in Ireland

MOKE

There is one that has long defied interpretation. This is Moke. It did not appear in print until after Donkey – not until 1840, in fact, when it was still often spelt Moak. Eric Partridge explains that it has no connection with any of the foregoing, and that we owe it to the Gipsies. One might have guessed that they would be involved in the affair sooner or later! Specifically to the Welsh Gipsies, in whose language *mokhio* means an ass. This Welsh Gipsy term is derived from the general Romany word *moila* or *meila*, having the same meaning as, and probably going back to, the Latin word *mulus*, for the interpretation of which no prize is offered.

Anthony Dent
Donkey: The Story of the Ass from East to West 1972

THE ONAGER

The ONAGER is said to be the Wild Ass. The Greeks to be sure, called the Ass 'on' and they called wild 'agra'. Africa breeds the creatures – large and untameable and wandering about in the desert.

One male at a time presides over the herds of females. When little males are born, the fathers get jealous of them and remove their testicles with a bite – for fear of which, the mothers hide them in secret places.

Physiologus says of the Wild Ass that, when twenty-five days of March have passed, it brays twelve times in the night and the same number in the day. From this the season is recognized as the 'Equinox' and people can tell, hour by hour, the time of day or night by counting the brays of the ass.

Now the Devil is symbolized by this animal, for he brays about the place night and day, hour by hour, seeking his prey. He does this when he knows night and day to be equal, i.e. when he knows that the number of those who walk in darkness is equal to the sons of light. For the Wild Ass does not bray unless it wants its dinner. As Job says, "Doth the Wild Ass bray when he hath grass?" Wherefore the Apostle also: "Our adversary the Devil, as a roaring lion, walketh about, seeking whom he may devour".

T. H. White
The Book of Beasts
A Translation of a 12th Century Bestiary

ABOUT THE ASS

The Ass is originally a native of hot and dry countries, and surely of all quadrupeds, one of the most genuine inhabitants of the desart, from his ability to subsist upon the most scanty herbage. In his wild state, like the hog, he is comparatively speedy, even fierce and courageous, and the natural enemy or rival of the horse. Even the domesticated Ass shews a kind of savage fierceness and resolution, in defence of her foal. For a certain attribute of the male Ass, a chapter of Ezekiel may be consulted. To dilate on the patience and submission of the domestic Ass, under whatever may occur, would be an attempt to illumine the sun: he is a true fatalist, an optimist, wedding all events, good or bad, for better or for worse; taking with the patience of a Stoic all the blows the heaviest hand can lay upon him, and deliberately waiting for the residue to come. The *Flemish* School of Painters and our *Gainsborough* have awarded the palm of picturesque beauty to the Ass; his gravity and sapient aspect had long before introduced him into the Commissions of the Peace. To be yet more serious, we declare on experience and as *Amateurs*, he is not that stupid and senseless animal which ignorance and cruelty represent him; on the contrary, his sagacity is eminent, and his affection and gratitude warm and lively, when adequately excited. Slavery and tyranny brutalize equally the *man* and the *ass*. The flesh of the wild Ass is highly esteemed as venison, in his native desarts, and we have lately heard of a *Nacker's* servant, who fares sumptuously whenever an Ass comes to the shop. But refined and pampered as the Europeans are, and scorning Ass-flesh, the most delicate ladies find Ass-milk a most pleasant and salubrious beverage. To conclude on his uses of this nature, a whole ass in abstract or metaphysic, subserves various purposes of literature, logical, metaphorical, and metonymical: in parts, his skin for example, hard and elastic, serves to give sound to drums, profit and chicanery to lawyers, and a stamp to corrupt Governments, through the medium of parchment; and being well tanned, makes shoes and boots equal in durability, to those *well-soaled* ones, with which that most skilful of operators *Homer* of old, shod his heroes.

The horrible treatment of the Ass, in our religious Country, exceeds, in profligacy, everything by comparison, excepting our treatment of the horse, which is still worse in degree, as the horse exceeds the ass in stature. In our youth, we saw with a shudder of indignant abhorrence, which now vibrates within us, a young miscreant mounted on an ass, booted and spurred; the ass seemed dull and regardless of the spur, and the ignorant or naturally hard-hearted urchin, dismounting and taking out his penknife, actually made an incision in each side of the depressed and toil-worn animal, into which, being remounted, he inserted the rowels of his spurs! We have even known asses advertised to be baited with *Bull-dogs*, under no question of *senatorial* approbation! Impartial justice, however, compels us to adduce facts of an opposite and consoling nature, although unfortunately of a more limited extent. Some few of the lowest class of labourers, our *blackguards*, to wit, are not only very kind, but excessively attached, to their asses, and the kindness and attachment are mutual. The present writer in his youth, walking in company with a medical friend through the Borough High Street, observed a great crowd collected, the occasion of which was, the mare-Ass of a pannier-man, who appeared much in the *flash*-line, had fixed her fore foot in a plug-hole, and was unable to extricate it; nor could her master, with his utmost exertions. The fellow blubbered like a great girl, outdid even the renowned Sancho Panza in lamentations for the loss of his Ass, and harangued the surrounding crowd on her virtues, until exhausted in matter and in breath, and lifting up his arms in the true style of natural or heaven-born orators, he exclaimed as his finale – "d– my eyes but she is an excellence!" *Demosthenes* himself, in his most passionate mood, could not have worked a greater effect upon his audience. A general burst of laughter and applause ensued from among the by-standers, and their zeal to serve this tender-hearted Ass-driver was inkindled in a moment, and to such good effect, that they shortly released the animal uninjured, and more than that, a collection of pence and sixpences ensued, from the example of my friend, which amply repaid the fellow for his loss of time.

Many of these animals are known to inhabit the miserable dwellings of their keepers, in the same close state of family society, as the *Arabian* horses . . . and to be particularly kind and attached to the children, looking into their faces with a fond and anxious solicitude, when they are moaning or wailing under any kind of suffering. It sometimes happens that, asses are turned out by the poor, at the close of the evening, in the grazing season, to feed through the night, upon the trespassing principle; the sagacious brutes, as if sensible of the trespass, are invariably found, by dawn of day, knocking with the fore foot at the door of their master's hut.

The humble Ass and his slow and patient labours, and trifling cost either for purchase or keep, seems to have been overlooked in this country, until the reign of Elizabeth, in the course of which asses came into common use. They have never been equally so in *Scotland*, nor in the Northern parts of Europe, probably because they are not proportionally useful with the native ponies in those cold regions. They remained with us a neglected and despised, although common animal, until the urgency of public circumstances not only introduced them to greater and more general attention, but even elevated their race to high honours, of which even the highest bred Courser of the

An 18th century print of an ass race

Desart might be proud. War, the eternal delight of Englishmen, and taxes, their glorious boast, had thinned the family of horses, and raised their price and expences to an insupportable height. The Ass, in meek and humble guise, now presented himself, and was universally accepted, in all cases wherein his substitution could be made available. He became the common country *express*, the orderly *riding-horse* of the farm; asses were driven four in hand, in the Stage Cart, and even in the Curricle: but his honours were derived from the fair and the gay, to whom he became the constant *pad*; and ladies of the highest rank visitant at *Bath*, *Brighton* and *Tunbridge*, employed tall and proper men to whip their asses through the streets and over the hills. *Balaam* of old, who was a Prince as well as a Prophet, rode upon an Ass; and old *Jack Bannister*, a prophet of another description, in his latter days, rode his Ass through the streets and squares of *London*.

The Earl of Egremont, long renowned for his splendid style of living, and for his hospitalities; his extensive establishment for breeding the horse, in which he nobly emulates the most illustrious Princes and Heroes of Antiquity, and his exquisite judgment in that animal; among his other numerous experiments, made a successful trial of Asses to cart coals upon the road. To speak of the Ass as a hackney, his rate upon the road, even in high condition, is seldom more than six miles per hour; yet such a defect of

speed could not well be presupposed from his figure: the shoulder of the Deer also is upright. There have been solitary examples of Asses which were *goers*. In the year 1763, we well remember to have seen at Mr. Samuel Taylor's, the then Stage Coach Master at *Colchester*, the Ass, which for the two previous years, successively, had carried the post-boy with the Mail, between that town and the Metropolis, a distance of fifty-one miles. He was a common bred English Ass, but of good size. We have been further informed, authentically or otherwise, that, many years since, an Ass was matched to run one hundred miles in twelve hours, over the *Round Course*, *Newmarket*, which he performed, incited thereto by a mare going before him, which he had covered the previous day. One of the chief recommendations of the Ass, is his ability to do moderate labour upon such unexpensive keep. But his performances would be of far greater account, if well fed with corn, and his size and ability to labour might be greatly increased, were it thought worth-while to improve his breed; in opposition to which, it is urged that, to improve his breed would be to detract from his utility, as after incurring nearly the expence of a horse, you would at last obtain but an Ass.

Anonymous
1776

IN YOUTH AND OLD AGE

The ass is fair of shape and of disposition while he is young and tender, ere he pass into age. For the elder the ass is, the fouler he waxeth from day to day, and hairy and rough, and is a melancholy beast that is cold and dry, and is therefore kindly, heavy and slow, and lusty, dull and witless and forgetful. Natheless he beareth burdens and may away with travail and thralldom, and useth vile meat and little, and gathereth his meat among briars and thorns and thistles.

Bartholomaeus Anglicus
On the Properties of Things c.1250

A KIND OF MUSIC

. . . The goodly sweet and continuall brayings, whereof they form a melodius and proportionable kind of musicke. Nor thinke I that any of our immoderate Musicians can deny but that their song is full of exceeding pleasure to be heard: because therein is to be discerned both concord, discord, singing in the meane, the beginning to sing in large compasse, then following into a rich fall . . . to hear the musicke of five or six voyces changed to so many of Asses is amongst them to heare a song of world without end.

The Noblenesse of the Ass
16th century

EQUUS ASINUS (The Donkey): The hoarseness of its voice, or bray, depends upon two small peculiar cavities situated at the bottom of the larynx.

Baron Cuvier
The Animal Kingdom Arranged in Conformity with its Organisation 1817

Every Ass Loves to Hear himself bray.

Thomas Fuller
Gnomologia: Adagies and Proverbs, 1732

THE NIGHTINGALE OF BRUTES

The ass, approaching next, confess'd
That in his heart he lov'd a jest:
A wag he was, he needs must own,
And could not let a dunce alone:
Sometimes his friend he would not spare,
And might perhaps be too severe:
But yet, the worst that could be said,
He was a *wit* both born and bred;
And, if it be a sin or shame,
Nature alone must bear the blame:
One fault he hath, is sorry for't,
His ears are half a foot too short;
Which could he to the standard bring,
He'd show his face before the king:
Then for his voice, there's none disputes
That he's the nightingale of brutes.

Jonathan Swift
The Beasts' Confession 1722

CONFORMATION, POINTS AND TYPE OF DONKEY

HEAD
Short rather than long, muzzle very small and tapering, the flesh soft and very delicate, profile concave ('dished'). The whole light and very pleasing.

JAWS
Generous, round and widely open.

EYES
Of good size, set low and wide apart.

EARS
To be well and firmly set, of good shape, and size in proportion to the donkey as a whole.

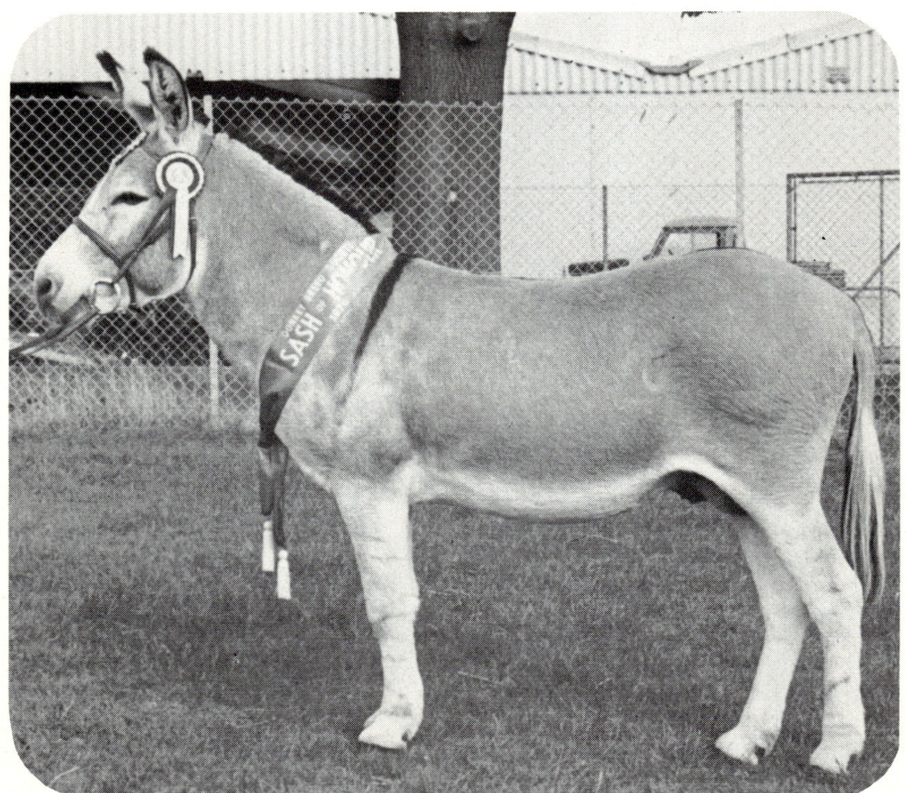

'Ascension', winner of eight championships, 1967–69

NECK

Within reason, the longer the better and to join both head and shoulder correctly. The top line and the underside to be straight showing no sign of concavity. The whole to be firm, well fleshed and carried without drooping.

BODY

Withers practically non-existent but if noticeable so much the better. The line of back to be practically level and reasonably short. A little concavity permitted in age, tendency to roach back a fault. The more oblique the shoulder, the better. The ribs to be well sprung – the deeper the girth the better.

QUARTERS

Long, wide, flat and generously fleshed with plenty of length between point of hip and point of buttock.

TAIL

Set strong and high.

FEET

All to be even and of good shape, hard in appearance, 'clean' and smooth of surface. The size must be adequate to the donkey and be true to the typical donkey hoof with no tendency to a low heel.

ACTION

To be level and true at walk and trot, smart, light and active.

SIZE

There is no limit, type and presence being essential. For description only the Society authorises the following terms:

Miniature: Under 9 hands.

Small Standard: 9 hands to 10 hands.

Standard: Over 10 hands to 11 hands.

Large Standard: Over 11 hands.

All measurements to be made without shoes.

LIMBS

All to be straight and true with adequate bone in proportion to type. Knees flat and wide, cannon bones short. Hocks set as low as possible, clean and correct in shape. Fore and hind-legs not too close, nor too wide apart. The fore-legs to show no sign of being back-of-the-knee (calf knee) nor the hind to show sickle or turned-in (cow hocks).

GENERAL NOTE: The donkey being a friendly, loveable and "family" animal judges will have this in mind and are advised (all things being equal) to consider favourably, and place accordingly, any donkey which has these attributes.

R. S. Summerhays

Issued by the Donkey Show Society (later the Donkey Breed Society) for the information of Judges, Owners and Breeders in 1968.

COLOUR

Most people think you can get brown donkeys or grey donkeys. So you can, but donkeys come in a much greater variety of colours than that. Here horse language does let one down a bit, because horses are not found in some shades which occur in donkeys, and therefore no names exist for them. Let us start simply. A grey donkey is one that is grey all over. It may be so pale as to be almost white, or it may be sooty and almost black. Its cross may be dark brown, darker grey or black. Occasionally donkeys have muzzles the same colour as the body, but a paler muzzle – mealy, pale grey or white – is usual. Some donkeys have dark, sooty muzzles, and almost all have white tummies. A brown donkey is brown all over. It may be light brown, mid-brown or dark brown. If it is dark brown you will find it difficult to see its cross. Scientifically, the cross on a donkey is related to the stripes on a zebra, and almost all donkeys have it. I have, in fact, owned one that did not. She was an elderly, bright strawberry roan mare with no trace of a dorsal stripe or line across her shoulders. In every other respect she was a typical donkey. Incidentally, the hair of the cross has a slightly different texture from the hair on the rest of the body, and this can be felt quite distinctly if you ever clip a donkey. Donkeys sometimes have rings of dark hair round their fore-legs and zebra-like markings may be present on the hind-quarters or back legs. The dorsal stripe on a zebra does not run up its mane, and the animal has rings on its tail. Otherwise the cross on a donkey is very similar to one of the stripes on a zebra.

Grey and brown are the two basic coat colours. Black donkeys should be so black that no trace of brown can be seen. These usually have grey or mealy muzzles and white tummies like other donkeys, but sometimes are black all over. Most donkeys are paler in their winter coats, but the true black donkey is black all the year round.

White donkeys are common in Egypt, but you do not see many in the British Isles. A white donkey is really an exceedingly pale grey, with a pale grey cross, black hooves and eyes which are normal in colour. A donkey which is devoid of any colour pigment is an albino, and will have white hooves and pink eyes. All white animals have a tendency towards deafness, but very little research has been done in connection with this subject, and none of it, as far as I know, on donkeys.

"Roan" is any colour, other than light grey, where the coat is flecked with single white hairs. Horses may be strawberry roan or blue roan; donkeys of all shades may be partly or wholly flecked. I call a donkey roan if it is only partly flecked, but my horsey friends tell me I am wrong.

Captain Hayes, in *Points of the Horse*, wrote that chestnut donkeys never occur. He was wrong, but it is a rare colour. I have only ever seen four chestnut donkeys, and I own all of them. Even the smartest horseman will admit that when he says chestnut he really means ginger. Chestnut just sounds better. Where a horse or donkey really is chestnut, that rich mahogany colour, you call it brown. Incidentally, a brown horse with black mane and tail is called a bay. Anyway, we should refrain from talking about ginger donkeys. One of mine is so rich in colour that I do not think I am exaggerating if I say she is rust-red. One pretty little miniature with a thick coat is certainly ginger, but if her coat is parted a greyish tinge may be seen underneath, an unlikely thing to find under what is, after all, basically a brownish colour. She does not shed her coat easily in the spring and in summertime suffers from the hot weather. The first spring that I clipped her out I had a nasty shock. I found I had a pile of bright ginger hair on the floor, and a slender little grey donkey who strolled off to tell her friends all about it. She has white hooves, and the most glamorous red eye-lashes. You will be glad to know that her new coat grew through the same colour as before.

A paler colour than chestnut can only be described as pink. I have never been troubled by pink elephants, but pink donkeys are very much a reality. Generally, pink donkeys are pale chestnuts flecked with grey or white – chestnut or pink roans in fact. A darker brown roan which still has a reddish tinge would be a strawberry roan. My large chestnut mare had a foal which was bright brown, somewhat reddish, but not a chestnut. He was almost the colour of treacle, and we called him by that name.

Brighter even than this is a pale colour which I can only call apricot. I had a particularly pretty apricot foal some years ago, but unfortunately she died when only a month old. Grey donkeys may have brown tips to their ears, in keeping with the colour of the cross, and I have one grey whose ears are apricot all over, and another, grey with an apricot head. Paler again in the same spectrum is an oatmealy sort of colour. This is not uncommon in donkeys, and I call it oatmeal.

Broken-coloured donkeys were never heard of until recently, but at present there is a great vogue for them, and a well-marked broken-coloured donkey will fetch an extremely fancy price, even if its conformation is bad and its temper worse. 'Broken-coloured' is a group term, including "piebald", "skew-bald" and "appaloosa". A piebald is a horse or donkey which has large areas of black and white interspaced. A skewbald is one which has large areas of any other colour and white, but is not to be confused with a roan, since white hairs should not occur in the other colour. Gypsy horses are often skewbald, and drum horses of the Household Cavalry are magnificent examples. Broken-coloured donkeys are usually of a more washy colour, with the white predominating. One white patch on a donkey or a horse does not make it broken-coloured, and donkeys with irregular patches leading off their bellies are not uncommon. Such donkey mares are sought after, as mated to a broken-coloured stallion they may produce a well-marked broken-coloured foal. Dealers often refer to broken-coloured donkeys as merely "coloured donkeys". An appaloosa is a white donkey with many distinct small black marks which are of thicker hair than the body coat.

Dappled grey donkeys are unusual, but not especially sought after. A dappled grey has darker grey circles in the coat, particularly on the hind

Drawing by Edwin Landseer R.A., 1802–1873

quarters. This is quite common with grey horses and standard on rocking-horses. Where any animal has been bred with colour as the chief consideration, that colour is very often achieved at the expense of a loss of conformation. This is seen very clearly in certain breeds of dogs. Even though so little has been done so far in the breeding of donkeys, the same tendency has already appeared, and any broken-coloured stallion, whatever his temperament and shape, commands a fee higher than a plain coloured donkey.

Robin Borwick
People with Long Ears, 1965

PERFECTION

Is there anything so resolved, disdainful, contemplative, solemn and serious as an ass?

Michel de Montaigne
16th century

SMELL

A donkey smells different. People who suffer from asthma or who are allergic to horses usually find that they are not affected by a donkey. A wet donkey smells different from a wet horse, and so does a hot, sweaty one. Incidentally, donkeys do not seem to sweat to nearly the same extent. All this is probably to do with the texture of the coat, but a horse's smell is always stronger and more pungent and attracts more flies. Nature has equipped a horse with a fly-switch at each end and muscles which may be twitched voluntarily in between. These anti-fly protections are absent in the donkey, who uses his mane and tail merely as adornments. Donkeys are troubled by flies, but not as much as horses, although some will rub their eyes against the insides of their fore-legs to remove the pests, and in the process make their faces quite sore. This, of course, only encourages the flies.

Some passionate horse lovers will tell you that they love the smell of a horse and even of a stable. Personally I prefer the smell of a donkey, but then I am prejudiced, as all my friends tell me.

Robin Borwick
People With Long Ears 1965

SAGACITY

The Ass is very susceptible of education: it has all the requisite qualities, delicate senses and an excellent memory; it remembers all the roads it has travelled and its timidity prevents it from taking others willingly. It fears water, to which however it may gradually become accustomed. If its eyes are covered, it refuses to proceed, and if overloaded it will accelerate its pace and go on until it falls . . . . But for the Horse, it would certainly have been the first of our domestic animals; our attention would have developed in it new qualities and improved the old. The Wild Horse and the Wild Ass are very nearly the same size; their strength is equal and their disposition not much different. It may even be said the Ass has more solid good qualities than the Horse. But the intelligence of the latter is greater and has gained the superiority which it ought. Brute strength should have no proportion in esteem, in comparison of intellectual power. . . .

Baron Cuvier
The Animal Kingdom arranged in Conformity with Its Organisation 1817

THE MIND OF A DONKEY

Donkeys, although their faces may belie it, are almost all endowed with a sense of humour, sometimes mischievous but rarely malevolent; and all, without exception, have definite characteristics of their own. In our establishment, which has ranged up to nearly twenty donkeys, I can recall some trait peculiar to every animal. The specialist in practical jokes is MeMoke, the "Wit" and our "Head Donkey", as visiting children call her. She really is the head donkey, as most of the others follow her example on matters of daily life, choosing which part of their range they will graze in the morning, coming to the gate to stare hopefully at the house, and lining up for hay rations. As I have said, MeMoke has an original turn of mind which was first demonstrated when we had had her only a short time. My husband was talking to her across a barbed wire fence when she suddenly leaned over and took his tie firmly between her teeth and then quite deliberately backed away. When my husband had been stretched as far as was possible without actual injury, the donkey stopped. There she stood with a sort of smile on her face and the tie still between her teeth. After a minute or two she allowed her victim to go. When strangers are in the field engrossed with any donkey but her, she will get behind women members of the party, and put her nose under their coats or skirts and then raise it sharply; she will do this repeatedly unless notice is taken of her, quite plainly appreciating the squeaks of dismay. With men she simply butts from behind, quite gently but with insistence. MeMoke always spots a gate which has been left open, can stretch her neck right over any fence to sample some garden shrub which had been considered quite out of reach, appropriates the largest portion of hay, etc.! Despite all this she is a steadying influence on the small herd, never losing her head, for instance, if some hysterical dog gets into the field and starts chasing – in fact he will soon find himself the one chased. The others look to her as the leader, and she has a reputation to keep up.

One of our most loveable donkeys is Mavourneen. She is not so "classy" as some of the others, but is so wonderful with children that she has had to be kept among the select breeding herd – as one breeds for temperament as well as for looks. The only trouble with Mavourneen is that if a fuss isn't made of her regularly, she sulks and will stand with her ears flat out on each side of her head if she feels neglected or too much attention is paid to another.

This Jenny's rival with children is a young pure white Jenny, who equally cannot bear to be passed over by them. Because of her unusual appearance, they often do choose her for preference, to Mavourneen's discomfiture, and she follows visitors with small children about persistently until one of them is put on her back.

We have only owned one donkey that seemed to have no sense of fun at all, and she was old and bore the marks of hard treatment. Jenny was "not amused" by anything, and gave her foals an excellent but very strict up-bringing – never hesitating to give them a hard nip if they became too rumbustious.

Donkeys make very deep friendships with each other and sometimes with ponies or horses. The particularly nervous Jenny was watched over and faithfully guarded for some time by an aged grey pony until he had to be taken to another field. Both had been bought at the same horse fair from different owners and can never have met before – the donkey, who was about a year old, belonging to a batch that had come from Ireland. They travelled together in the same horse box to our home and were inseparable until the little donkey got used to new donkey friends and the pony went off to live with a horse.

The friendship can be between more than two. We have, for instance, what is known as "the Gang". This consists of four donkeys – the stallion and three young Jennies. They are always to be seen together whether sheltering or grazing, and join forces in trying to establish rights over as much of whatever kind of food is going as possible. On one occasion, when being transferred from one field to another by means of droving, which happens not infrequently, the Gang made a bid for freedom and bolted off into the woodland which surrounds our home. Having got the rest of the herd safely into the field, I spent the rest of the afternoon searching for them without success. We were considerably worried, as the woods abound in yew trees. The following morning a friend, who is skilled in woodcraft, set off on a tracking expedition. He did eventually run the donkeys down a mile or so away at the entrance to our local prep school, where they would presumably have had a warm reception. They all looked thoroughly smug and were most unwilling to turn their steps int the direction of home. As their conductor had taken only one halter, the return journey proved very trying and only their refusal to be parted made it possible.

The humourless Jenny, mentioned above, was the only donkey we have had who appeared not to mind being alone. When without a foal, you would find her standing dreaming by herself, doing nothing in particular by the hour. I must add that she is now retired and has gone to live with two kind ladies who heap her with all the comforts a donkey could want on earth.

M. R. de Wesselow

Donkeys: Their Care and Management 1967

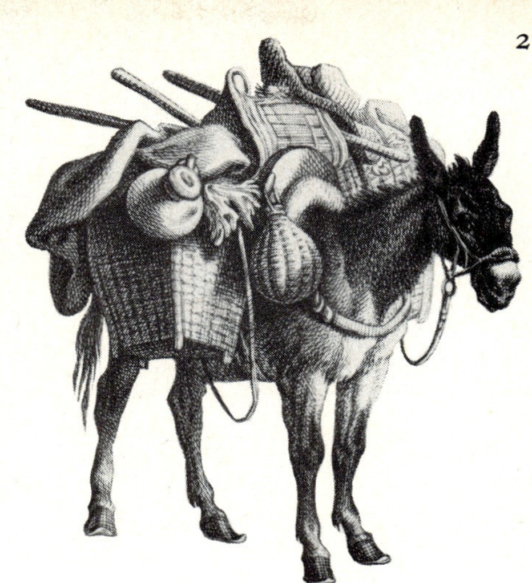

DONKEY

He belongs under a blow-torch sky
as much as selling water, or carrying beds through the street
or endlessly standing around;
he with big dirty hearthrug head and gorgeous eye,
he with his stripe of vigour, who raging in the heat
and belly-ache of love throws bitter complaint out with the sound
of croup, of cars braking, of hinges, a last-ditch cry.

Ankling along the cobbles of a cliffside, breakneck street
or the tracks of the bald plains or spinbrain mountain-twists,
he has come to a peace with servitude and those by whom he is downed;
let us waive further pathos, as he would;
for him there is no defeat:
turds entice him, but mostly he dreams straight on (and his ankles
are tiny like children's wrists.)

Hung with cheap lines of pottery,
bashed milk-cans, brushes, prayer-rugs or kindling wood,
taken for granted, loved or merely used,
with the master piled amid,
he props the four-hooved beast-and-human pyramid
that though stone yielded has withstood,
and points up over the early bones,
relic and monument . . .
donkey on business, treading the weeds past side-pitched pillar-drums
– pillars of the lost, imperial, the earthquake-tumbled towns.

Bernard Spencer
With Luck Lasting 1963

2. Donkeys Diverse

THE DONKEYS OF THE COSTERMONGERS

The costermongers almost universally treat their donkeys with kindness. Many a costermonger will resent the ill-treatment of a donkey as he would a personal indignity. These animals are often not only favourites, but pets, having their share of the coster-monger's dinner when bread forms a portion of it, or pudding, or anything suited to the palate of the brute. Those well-used manifest fondness for their masters and are easily manageable; it is, however, difficult to get an ass, whose master goes regular rounds, away from its stable for any second labour during the day, unless it has fed and slept in the interval. The usual fare of a donkey is a peck of chaff, which costs 1d., a quart of oats and a quart of beans, each averaging 1½d., and sometimes a pennyworth of hay, being an expenditure of 4d. or 5d. a day; but some give double this quantity in a prosperous time. Only one meal a day is given. Many costermongers told me that their donkeys lived well when they themselves lived well.

"It's all nonsense to call donkeys stupid" said one costermonger to me, "them's stupid that calls them so: they're sensible. Not long since I worked Guildford with my donkey-cart and a boy. Jack (the donkey) was slow and heavy in coming back until we got in sight of the lights at Vauxhall-gate, and then he trotted on like one o'clock, he did indeed! just as if he smelt it was London besides seeing it, and he knew he was at home. He had a famous appetite in the country and the fresh grass did him good. I gave a country lad 2d. to mind him in a green lane there. I wanted my own boy to do so, but he said, "I'll see you further first". A London boy hates being by himself in a lone country part. He's afraid of being burked; he is indeed. One can't quarrel with a lad when he's away with one in the country; he's very useful. I feed my donkey well. I sometimes give him a carrot for a luxury, but carrots are dear now. He's fond of mashed potatoes and has many a good mash when I can buy them at 4 lbs. a penny."

Henry Mayhew
Mayhew's London 1851

REMEMBRANCE OF THINGS PAST

What's happened to the medical profession? What are our doctors about nowadays? Time was, and I remember this very well, when it was quite a common occurrence for the doctor to prescribe asses' milk for delicate patients. We never hear of this today.

It may surprise many to learn that there were a number of milkmen (I suppose that would be the proper description), at any rate a number of traders who kept herds of donkeys for this particular purpose. I remember one particularly big concern who operated I think from somewhere in North London who made a regular delivery of asses' milk in the West End of London. I don't know whether my memory is indulging in some flight of fancy when I say I seem to remember actually seeing a donkey being milked outside a house in some London Square – a pleasant touch of rural life! Perhaps a substitute has been found for this health-restoring milk of Victorian days, something in tablet or tin.

R. S. Summerhays
1970

THE MILK OF HUMAN KINDNESS

Once on a time a certain English lass
Was seized with symptoms of such deep decline,
Cough, hectic flushes, ev'ry evil sign,
That, as their wont is at such desperate pass,
The Doctors gave her over – to an ass.

According, the grisly Shade to bilk,
Each morning the patient quaff'd a frothy bowl
Of asinine new milk,
Robbing a shaggy suckling of a foal
Which got proportionately spare and skinny –
Meanwhile the neighbours cried "poor Mary Ann!
She can't get over it! She never can!"
When lo! to prove each prophet was a ninny
The one that died was the poor wet-nurse Jenny.

To aggravate the case,
There were but two grown donkeys in the place;
And most unluckily for Eve's sick daughter,
The other long-ear'd creature was a male,
Who never in his life had given a pail
Of milk, or even chalk and water.
No matter: at the usual hour of eight
Down trots a donkey to the wicket-gate,
With Mister Simon Gubbins on its back, –
"Your sarvent, Miss, – a werry spring-like day, –
Bad time for hasses tho'! good lack! good lack!
Jenny be dead, Miss, – but I'ze brought ye Jack,
He doesn't give no milk – but he can bray".

So runs the story,
And, in vain self-glory,
Some Saints would sneer at Gubbins for his blindness –
But what the better are their pious saws
To ailing souls, than dry hee-haws,
Without the milk of human kindness?

Thomas Hood
From: *Ode to Rae Wilson, Esq. 1837*

WALLY ON MARGATE BEACH

When my father was three, he was taken by his two elder brothers to watch the concert party on the beach at Broadstairs. Halfway through the show members of the audience were invited on the stage to do a turn. Pushed forward by his brothers, my father amazed the assembled holiday makers with two verses of *If I Could Plant a Tiny Seed of Love.* He received tumultuous applause and a stick of rock. Afterwards his brothers treated him to a donkey ride, while his parents in their holiday finery watched anxiously from the promenade.

My mother too has a fund of childhood seaside memories – of stepping off the train at Ramsgate straight on to the beach, of hilarious mixed bathing parties (to judge by the photographs, those big black cotton one-piece bathing costumes revealed a jolly sight more than the skimpiest of today's bikinis), and of the familiar faces of the characters who returned year after year for the summer season – the donkey boy, the gipsy fortune teller, the promenade photographer, the Punch and Judy man.

Sadly, over the years, the bingo halls, foreign package holidays and a general shortage of spending money have conspired to force most summer season folk out of business. But many still pop up every year and help to maintain that traditional English seaside spirit which otherwise might have become just a vague memory in the minds of a few older people, like a well-thumbed album of faded holiday snaps.

Wally Jordan, for instance, has been a donkey boy for 49 years. I found him sitting with his donkeys under the shade of the sundeck on Margate beach, waiting patiently for the tide to go out. Actually, the donkeys belong to Mr. Brown, a timber merchant for whom Wally works in the winter. For many years Brown's Donkeys have been giving children rides up and down Margate beach, but Wally is doubtful if they can continue much longer. "Well, there's no money about, is there? And what there is has gone abroad."

One donkey, anxious to see some action, starts to wander off. "Where are you off to, Winston?" shouts Wally. "You'll get the sack, you will". The donkey stops and appears to fall asleep instantly on its feet. "He loves to work, does my Winston", explains Wally. "They all do. If one of them gets taken queer, you can't drag him off the sand. Well, its their life."

Clearly it's Wally's life too. He's deeply attached to his donkeys, won't give rides to children over a certain size, and those he does allow to climb on are treated more strictly than the donkeys themselves. "Children are all too spoiled these days", he grumbles. "In my young day, if you dared wander along the road to Cliftonville or Westgate, chances are a gentleman in a top hat and carrying a gold-topped cane would tell you to go back where you came from and call you a scruff."

A crowd of children gathers as he talks and the tide has retreated far enough to leave a narrow strip of hard wet sand. "All right," shouts Wally, "go on, get to work", and the donkeys turn and move sleepily into the sunshine, the children dancing alongside. "You've got to take what you can get these days", he calls out cheerfully, waving his cane.

Christopher Matthew
The Sunday Times 1971

If all men say thou art an ass then bray.

Thomas Draxe
A Treasury of Ancient Adagies and Sententious Proverbs 1616

IT ALL STARTED WITH JACK

Ron Brewer, Donkey Proprietor, is how you'd find me in the phone book, but hundreds of people, young and old, just call me the Donkey Man. I don't mind. Donkeys are my life, and I wouldn't change it for any other.

These days I always keep a stock of thirty or forty animals, mostly donkeys but a few Shetland ponies, which do all kinds of jobs in all kinds of places. One week a donkey may be giving rides at Wormwood Scrubs. The next week he may be acting in a film over at Elstree – and begging chocolate off the stars when the camera isn't on him.

Besides taking my donkeys and ponies to all sorts of events from school fêtes to West End pantomimes, I'm a dealer too, and every year scores of animals pass through my hands to owners in this country and on the Continent. And I breed donkeys as well. There's a lot more to the donkey business than taking sixpences at the seaside. But it all started over twenty years ago with one donkey – Jack.

If you go out to my field today you'll see Jack. He's quite an old man now as donkeys go – over thirty. He cost me £7, but I wouldn't part with him for a thousand pounds.

I say it started with Jack, but in a way it began long before I had him.

My father kept horses, hundreds of them. He bought and sold them, and hired them out for riding, and bred them. And he always kept a few donkeys to put with the foals. When a foal was a yearling it was taken away from its mother, but it was given a donkey for company. That kept it happy and stopped it straying to look for its mother.

Donkeys were the animals for me. They were the right size for a small boy. When I got a chance to help with the donkeys on the beach at Weston-super-Mare, near where we lived, I jumped at it.

For over 100 years Mrs. Drew's family had been keeping donkeys and ponies at Weston, for giving rides and pulling little carts on the sands. Business was brisk in the summer when the schools broke up and families poured into the town for their holidays, and Mrs. Drew was often in need of extra small boys to help out. So at the grand age of ten I started working for her and learning the donkey business the hard way – everything from giving the animals their morning feed and smartening them up for the beach to putting them back in their field last thing in the evening. It was tiring work for a small boy, but much better fun than school, and from Mrs. Drew I got a thorough grounding in the donkey trade which has stood me in good stead all my life.

And so those carefree summer holidays, long before the gathering clouds of World War II finally broke, saw me happy as a sand-boy – collecting the sixpences, picking up the kids who went too fast and fell off, and dreaming of the day when I would have donkeys of my own.

When I was old enough I came up to London to work. War broke out and I expected to be called up into the Forces, but I was found to be medically unfit and so I did agricultural work instead. The time eventually came when I could give that up and achieved my ambition at last.

I looked around and found a field I could rent. I went to Southall market and paid my £7 for Jack. I was in the donkey business.

There weren't many donkeys in London during those war years, so Jack and I had plenty of work to keep us busy. Billy Smart had a fair on Ealing Common at that time, and he agreed to let me give rides on Jack if in return I would help his boy with a pony and trap – a trap which I later bought and used constantly until last year.

Business was brisk, one donkey led to another, and by the time I left Smart's fair and started on my own I had six donkeys and four skewbald Shetland ponies.

I've bought and sold a lot of animals since then, but I've never considered parting with Jack. I know his ways and he knows mine. We've come this far together and we'll go on a good way yet.

People say donkeys are stupid and talk about "horse-sense", but in my view a donkey is more intelligent than a horse, and old Jack is as wise as any animal I've known. He's reliable too. If someone wants a donkey to bring Cinderella's coach safely on to a brightly lit stage, with crowds of performers and the orchestra playing fit to scare most animals out of their wits, Jack's the donkey for the job. He'll stop or start or turn with just a guiding hand on his bridle, as cool as an old trouper. He always has someone he knows on stage with him – one of the lads who helps me regularly, if I can't be there myself. Many's the time I've been togged up in a fancy costume and grease-paint so that my own mother wouldn't know me – but Jack does.

Jack's reliable in some other ways too. For instance, you can rely on him to get out from under certain sorts of rider. Put a baby on his back and he goes along as safe as a sofa. Put on anyone who's a bit cocky, who digs his heels in and plays the rough rider, and that boy is off before he knows what's happened. Up go Jack's heels, over his head sails the cocky boy, and then Jack looks at him on the ground and goes "Hee-haw" as if to say "There, I've done it. Have another go".

It's not only boys who have to be taught a lesson sometimes. I have girls as well as boys helping me in the summer, and if they've taken riding lessons they may think they know everything. But riding a donkey isn't like riding a horse – a donkey doesn't have the same sort of withers to grip with the legs. [SIC]

If I get a girl or boy who says, "Oh yes, I ridden *hundreds* of times", I point to Jack and say, "All right, ride that". Up the lane they go and I always know if there's been any monkey-business: Jack comes back by himself.

But he's not a vicious animal. He just insists on his rights. For instance, I don't allow anyone who weighs more than 8 stone to ride a donkey in a race. If I don't realize that a rider is over-weight, Jack soon tells me. He tips him straight off.

On one occasion his built-in weighing machine caused an embarrassing scene. I had taken him to a summer fête where one of the big attractions was a personal appearance by a popular film star. At one stage in the proceedings she was supposed to pose on the back of the donkey. Up she climbed in her dazzling dress, and as she settled herself on the saddle she muttered to me "Hold him, won't you, for goodness' sake!" The crowd cheered and clapped, and I must agree she looked marvellous. Her weight was arranged in all the proper places. Unfortunately it must have added up to more than 8 stone. Something distracted my attention and I accidentally let go of Jack's head. That was it – the next thing I knew, the actress was on the ground with her dress over her head and several hundred spectators were gazing at a fine spectacle not scheduled on the programme.

Another thing Jack won't put up with is a rider who carries a whip. One lad was taught this lesson in a way he won't forget.

I was standing by the gate of the field late one afternoon as the boys were bringing home the donkeys from some event. They came straggling down the lane and into the field one after the other, and last of all came Jack – with no rider. "Hello", I said, "where's Pitcher?" This was a boy who often helped me with the animals, and I knew he wouldn't have left Jack without good cause. The other boys couldn't tell me anything. The last time they'd seen Pitcher, he'd been sitting on Jack. I walked some way back along the lane and began to get worried when I could find no sign of the boy. Then I told myself not to start imagining things – he'd probably climbed down and let Jack go on alone while he went to sleep in a field, or something like that. I peered over the hedges, but there was no Pitcher asleep in the grass. There was no Pitcher anywhere. I was on the point of giving up the search when I heard a piping voice. "Here I am", said the voice. "Here I am". I walked over to where the sound was coming from. All I could see was a little pair of glasses looking over the edge of the ditch. But the rest of Pitcher was there too, soaked in ditch water, covered in mud, and stuck all over with thorns like a pin-cushion. And how had he got there? He had ignored my warnings and pulled a stick out of the hedge as he rode along. Jack spotted the stick. . . .

As you see, Jack is a donkey with a certain independence of spirit. I had further proof of this a year ago when people started phoning me to say that a

'Children Riding Donkeys on a Road' by Jacques Laurent Agasse 1767–1849

donkey was wandering round Southall. I picked up the receiver one day to hear a strange voice say, "Is that Mr. Brewer? You don't know me, but I live in such-and-such a road. I thought I'd better ring you because there's a donkey walking down the pavement." I jumped into the van and drove to the road where the caller lived. No donkey in sight. I drove around for a bit, looking for the vanished donkey, and then round the fields to check that one really was missing. I counted the donkeys carefully twice, and they were all there. The gates were firmly shut. A few days later the phone rang again. "Mr. Brewer" another voice said, "I've just given a slice of bread to a donkey that walked into my garden. He's gone away now, but perhaps you'd better come and look for him". Into the van again, and off to find the wandering donkey. And again there was no donkey that I could see walking about Southall, and all my animals were present and correct in their fields by the time I got there. After a while somebody explained the mystery to me. Passing by one of the fields one day, he'd seen a donkey put his front feet on the bottom strand of wire in the fence and, when it was pressed right down, push up the top wire with his neck and wriggle through. Then, smartly off down the lane towards the houses where he knew a soft-hearted housewife would give him the titbits he appreciated. And of course the donkey – it was Jack, as you might expect – would get back into the field in the same crafty way, which explained why his master found him there with all the others after wasting his time driving all round Southall. Still, I don't grudge him his walks as long as he doesn't cause any trouble. They're obviously important to him. The man who has the field next to mine saw Jack wandering off one day and, being a helpful fellow, drove him back into the field and shut the gate on him. That happened only once. He's met Jack outside the field several times since, and each time Jack has taken one look at him and galloped off at full speed in the opposite direction. He doesn't take long to learn.

His favourite walk is along the towpath which runs near his field. At about 7.30 in the morning he's often to be seen making his way along the path towards Hanwell. Off he goes, past the lock-keeper's cottage, ignoring the greetings of the bargees, who know him well by now, happily snuffing the morning air. And then back he comes for breakfast.

One morning something – perhaps a desire for wider travel – led him to the big garage at Hanwell where they keep the buses at night. He must have got bored with waiting for his journey to start, for an astonished conductress found him curled up, fast asleep, on the step of her bus. I'm surprised he didn't make straight for the top deck while he was about it – he's very handy at climbing stairs. Working at theatres often involves getting up and down tricky flights of steps back-stage, and several times he's been taken up to a bedroom to cheer up an invalid.

I used to worry about him wandering about on his own – not that I can stop him, it seems – but he never gets lost and he has excellent traffic sense. He recognizes a red light and won't go on till it turns green, and people have told me, though I've never seen it for myself, that he uses zebra crossings to go from one side of a busy road to the other.

The other day a friend mentioned to me a book published in 1870 called *The Adventures of a Donkey, written by himself*. Was it my "Clever Jack" he suggested, whose name was on the cover? Well, how *could* my Jack have written it? He may be old, but he's not *that* old.

Ron Brewer
Donkey Man 1964

AT THE RACES

Event 1 – "Donkey in Best Condition" – is billed for 11 o'clock and the first competitors, with wide ears, ruffled coats and diminutive appearance, draw appreciative "ums" and "ahas" from the crowd as they parade with their equally diminutive riders.

Official Race Cards are selling briskly in the car park which, under a blinding sun, is steadily building up into a shimmering Field of a Cloth of Chrome. "The Donkey Club would like to stress that . . . the primary object of the meeting must never be lost: to improve the status of the donkey in this country, and to ensure the welfare of this humble, misunderstood and often abused little animal."

As the morning draws on, the "events" proceed – a build-up for the races after lunch: "Donkey and Carrot", "Jumping Class", "Obedience Test" – for the uninitiated "obedience" apparently means leaning with all possible force against an animal intent on going the other way.

Bookies are feeling more daring and the legend "Each Way Betting All Races 2–1" is being rubbed off blackboards and more luring odds of 10–1 being offered. As Runners come under Starter's Orders for the first race parents heave and shove to keep the entries in order.

Then suddenly – at who knows what sign – they're off. Some sort of group hypnosis seems to grip the donkeys for, in spite of the altercations a few moments ago, they all go gambolling off in the same direction.

Their speed is considerable and there is little need to invoke Rule 9 ("No person shall be permitted to chase or employ any other artificial means whatsoever for the purposes of increasing the speed of a donkey . . .").

Stirrupless, the donkeys jolt out of sight round the bend to the hill up to the finish. The noise from the crowd is deafening as the field comes into sight

for the final 20 yards, donkeys swerving dangerously left and right. The leaders come on relentlessly but some outsiders take time off to speak with friends.

In the lead, the jockeys are white-faced with fatigue and can scarcely cry out words of encouragement as they approach the finish. The donkeys, however, are not even breathing heavily. Over the loudspeakers the official results are announced.

Half-an-hour until the next race and there is a surge of the crowd to the funfair where the sun flashes off the Victorian cut-glass of the roundabout with its flamboyant red message, "F. Harris & Sons present the Southdown Galloping Horses, the Most Pleasing Ride for All Ages."

Over the boundary that wandering thunder cloud known to every village fête the length and breadth of Britain looms up in the northern sky, broods for a time over the next field but then backs off towards some other rural event in Sussex.

By the penultimate race at 4.30 the outward bound cars are beginning to reach a steady flow; the money for charity is rattling in at a slower pace; the pile of unused ice-cream cones growing lower. But from the exits are leaving a great body of people who, surely, must all have slightly more affection for the "humble, misunderstood and so often abused little animal" – the donkey. Not everybody leaves immediately, however, for under the lengthening shadows of oak trees Mr. Harris's roundabout horses still gallop out into the summer night.

Tim Matthews
The Field 1971

THE RACING STABLE

With a gambling man's metallic discipline I let several races go by. Before going for broke I judiciously studied form.

In the Fetlock Frolics – sixth circuit of the course – I moved in for the kill. My bet was on Burp (by Spanish, out of Onion). The winner was Ripalong (by Getting, out of Gear).

Easy come, easy go. With a shrug and the twisted smile which marks the high plunger, I flipped away my 5p slip. However, it had not escaped my notice that Burp, a gunmetal beast bearded along its underparts, bore an uncanny resemblance to Modern Miss in the earlier PTA Handicap.

Moreover it had an extraordinary similarity to a contestant in the Wessex Stakes, Chump Chop.

The proceeds were for the neighbouring village school. One didn't ask awkward questions about assumed aliases and switched colours. The same six runners (zest noticeably waning) were being re-shuffled for the next Donkey Derby event.

I wandered over to the elegant varnished horsebox parked by the hedge. "Donkey Racing Team", said the notice on the rear. "Please Pass." Not very difficult, I thought, glancing back at the grim neck-and-neck struggle being fought out at a sluggish trickle inside the ring of straw bales.

On the van were the stars' portraits, painted on slices of tree trunk. Supernags, one and all. "Beauty, The Prettiest Marked Donkey in England"; "Snow White, Royal Command Performance"; "Delcia, Christened on TV, Celebrated by Champagne."

I recognised Beauty. I knew her as Burp. Her real name seemed to me a trifle extravagant. About Snow White's and Delcia's honorifics I wasn't quite clear. Still it could hardly be doubted that they had great lustre in donkey society.

How fortunate we were to have them in this quiet corner. These four-legged aces – swigs of bubbly, audiences of crowned heads – were used to the big time. What triumphal grand tours were marked by those placards . . . Skegness, Filey, Barry. No wonder Burp, with her supercilious mien, hadn't seemed to be trying in our rural capers.

Later, long after the skittle alley and Junior Big Dipper had been dismantled, we were driving home following a pub snack. The headlights touched a vehicle lumbering along the B-road. It was the Donkey Racing Team's mobile home. Inside, I suppose, were Delcia, Snow White and the rest, bound for the next roar of applause for their *haute école* in some far off gay resort. Between times, there was the truth of the glamorous life: a jawful of hay in the swaying darkness while rain splattered on the wooden roof.

Kenneth Allsop
Daily Mail 1971

"WASCHL"

Please excuse me my very poor English but English is not my mother tongue than I am German girl. The English language was in my school very needy and this letter is writes with help of a dictionary.

I have readed your book of the "Ulmers Tierbuchreihe". The title was "Esel, Freunde der Kinder" (donkeys friends of children).

I will tell you about my own donkey. The name of the donkey mare is "Waschl". Waschl means in the Bavarian dialect "long ear". In this Spring is Waschl three years old. Two years ago I have Waschl buyed. It is born in a donkey stud in Bavaria. It was very timided. Two weeks after this purchase is my donkey delivered of the stud-owner. In the intervall has my father his old hobbyroom was building. It is a wooden room and it is treble. In the middle room is Waschl's home. On its left is straw, leaves and its hay. In the other side are hay only. Waschl's apples and the other food is in father's new hobbyroom. In the winter time is donkey's stable right and left warm' The other sides are covered with straw.

You see that my donkey in the very cold Bavarian winter do not freeze in the night. Waschl hates the snow and its love no water. Our plot is border on a flowing water. One this side we use not fence. The willow of my donkey is very big. Its willow companions are six sheep and many hens. They are not its friends.

Waschl's exterior: Waschl is a "normal-donkey", its measure are about one meter. The colour of its skin is grew with brown basis colour. The cross and ears are grown. It is a pretty donkey. I can it not ride, it goes not under its rider (Puhhh English language is a very very hard language.) I believe that Waschl more joy on pulling of coaches and sledges.

Waschl is very obstinate. Twice we used the veterinary. But now is the donkey healthy. I am 20 years old and I am an enthusiastic rider. I say it gives no likely animals as donkeys and also horses. I will my Waschl never miss.

Please excuse many mistakes but the enthusiasm for your book I must write. There are no books about donkeys in Germany. I thank you for it. With many good wishes for the new year. Also many good wishes for your family. And greets your donkey.

from a letter to Robin Borwick 1972

DOGSTAR IN THE EAST

In an inconspicuous corner of the Horse Museum at Babolna there stands a little model, say three hands high, painted in natural colours, of a fine upstanding jackass. Now Babolna is Hungary's top establishment of this kind, it is totally dedicated to the horse in general and the Arab horse in particular. The graves of respected patriarchs of dynasties, O'bayyan, Shagya, Koheilan, Ghazal, lie thick in the garden outside, while beyond in the vast barns and the yards and the paddocks their descendants flourish like so many green bay trees or wicked men.

The statuette bore a label with the name SIRIUS, and something else, incomprehensible to me, in Hungarian. I asked the official interpreter, and the man from the Ministry of Agriculture who was showing us round and spoke German, and the Stud Manager who spoke rather less German, what it was all about, and why, especially, this jack had been called Dog Star. None of them would give me an answer, but simply chanted, in English and in German "Don-key, Don-key, Es-el; Es-el" as they passed on to the next exhibit, the skull of some noble oriental progenitor.

No light was shed on this mystery until the day before I was to leave Hungary, when I went to a village outside Budapest to see over the diplomatic livery stables. In the streets of the village I saw, first of all, a jennet, which has become a very rare sight in England, and later some pairs of mules in country wagons fetching coal from the station; the jennet was pulling the corporation dust cart. Rather fine mules. But I had previously had the impression that Hungary was not much of an ass-country, but rather one which until yesterday used horses where Mediterranean countries would have used mules.

I asked my guide therefore whether there was still any considerable mule-breeding, and its inevitable corollary, donkey-breeding, in Hungary. The answer was no, not for its own sake, but there is an irreducible minimum of mules which are a by-product. A by-product of what? In Hungary, the donkey is the mare-owner's last resort in cases of infertility. This is so even now that the majority of horses, and absolutely all the horses of quality, are state-owned. In the case of a valuable maiden mare who proves consistently barren to the horse, recourse is had to artificial insemination, not with horse semen but with donkey semen. If that is no go either, then the mare is covered with a jackass. This first hybrid pregnancy seldom fails to start the reproductive cycle rolling, and on the foal heat after dropping the mule foal the mare will in the majority of cases take the stallion and hold to the service. Hence the fact that a nucleus of breeding asses is maintained (this explains the jennet) and a certain number of mules are reared and used for harness work. In the nature of things some of these mules are of very high quality, because if the mare had not been something rather out of the ordinary it would not have been worth while, in a still horse-rich country like Hungary, to take all that trouble with her.

My friend was also able to throw some light on Sirius of Babolna. It seems that in the good old pre-1914 times he had been the friend of some very well-connected mares indeed who were shy breeders. And his name was a printer's error; once bestowed, according to an inflexible stud-book rule, it could not be altered, even by deed-poll. He was in fact brought home from the Orient by the Hungarian general Fedlallah el Hedad (1843–1924) whose story itself is a romantic one. Michael Fedlallah, to give him the name adopted at baptism, was a barefoot Bedouin boy of fourteen when the Austro-Hungarian commission under Colonel von Brudermann visited Arabia in the year of the Indian Mutiny; he went along with some horses which his father had sold to

the *faranghi*, as a groom, by land and sea, finally arriving at Lipizza. There the Emperor Francis Joseph came to inspect the purchase, took an interest in the boy, and had him sent to the imperial cadet school, from which he graduated in due course as a cornet of hussars. He eventually became a general of the remount service, and for long was commandant of Babolna, personally conducting further purchasing expeditions to the Near East. On the last of these, in 1901–02, he bought Sirius to serve at Babolna as the last hope of frustrated maternal instinct (the Bedouin had a good eye for a donkey before ever the first of them set eyes on a horse). The Dog Star label is the brain-child of some hamfisted signwriter – it ought to be *Siricus* – "The Syrian" – and all right-minded donkey people know that the cream of the cream of asinine society are the noble breed of Syria.

Anthony Dent
1973

DONKEY WHEELS AS A SOURCE OF POWER

In the winter of 1747–48 Pehr Kalm, a Swedish naturalist who had been a pupil of Linnaeus, came to England. He had been commissioned by the Swedish Government and Academy of Science to go to North America to see what plants might be worth introducing into the North of Europe from that part of the world. Kalm's journey took him first to London, and, while waiting for a ship to cross to America, he visited the Duke of Bridgewater's estate at Ashbridge Park, in Hertfordshire. The published account of his travels includes the following:

"The duke's house was situated on one of the chalk ridges of this place, where there was no spring to get good water out of. Therefore they had caused a well to be dug through the chalk ridge to a depth of very many fathoms (275 ft.). To get up the water out of the same, a large wheel was built, which had a thick axletree, around which there went a long rope which had a large bucket fastened to each end, yet in this way, that when the one pail went up with the water, the other went empty down. Inside the great wheel a horse was led, who by his walking inside the wheel drove it round, and thus the buckets were lifted up and down."

Kalm's account remains one of the only two descriptions from the era in which they were used of a donkey wheel, the commonest but not the only form of treadwheel crane. This is surprising since treadwheels, powered by human beings or animals, were common in Roman times and were still being constructed in England in the late 19th century. (There is in the Hampshire Village of Dummer, a charming little wheel, dated 1879, above a well which once served the community).

The donkey wheel met a special need common to the chalk hills of south-east England. In this region rainfall is rapidly absorbed and soon sinks to a considerable depth. Before the days of main water supply very deep wells of up to 300 ft. or more had to be sunk by communities and farms on the higher hills in order to reach the water level. Getting buckets up and down such wells by hand would have been a laborious and time-consuming job, which wooden treadwheels powered by animals would accomplish with ease. The use of donkey wheels for this purpose, first recorded definitely in England in 1587, must have become widespread, for more than 50 examples are recorded mostly in the Chilterns and the North and South Downs, but also as far afield as Devon and Yorkshire; 28 still exist, though only at Carisbrooke Castle can one see a treadwheel still being worked by donkeys. The area of their most intensive use may be indicated by a reference in an encyclopaedia of 1843 to "the Kentish fashion of the antlia, tread or crane-mill".

The surviving wheels vary greatly in size, from 10 to over 19 ft. in diameter, in part a reflection of the form of animal that drove them. The donkey (sometimes two donkeys) was much the commonest, but retriever dogs and one or even two men were used too. As we have seen, horses are reported to have been used at Ashridge Park, and Richard D'Acres in his book *The Art of Water-Drawing* (1650) refers rather contemptuously to great hollow wheels, hanging perpendicularly, in which men tread "but which are worked more efficiently by cattle and brute beasts". Donkey wheels are mostly to be found in farm buildings or in purpose-built well houses, but sometimes in dwelling houses, as at the Fox and Hounds Inn at Beauworth in Hampshire.

The bucket (or buckets) would be at the end of a rope leading directly from the wheel's axle, or a drum attached to it. In cases where the axle could not be erected immediately above the well, pulley wheels were necessary.

Donkey Wheel at Annable's Manor, Kinsbourne Green, Hertfordshire

Thomas Baskerville, referring to Ashridge in 1681, gives a graphic account of how the water would be delivered: as soon as the bucket came above the collar of the well a man emptied it into a leaden cistern and at that moment "the horse turns himself in the wheel without bidding or forcing and travels the other way to draw up the next bucket, and so this water after it has served all the offices of the house runs into the pond". A refinement at Greys Court were two iron hooks attached to the cistern which caught the buckets and automatically tipped them over.

Brakes were generally needed to prevent the bucket from returning rapidly to the bottom of the well after it had been raised, a task that might take up to 15 minutes. A variety of brakes were designed for this purpose, some applied to the axle, some across the outside of the treads and others, in the form of metal straps, to part of the circumference of the wheel. The basic design of donkey wheels is much like that of water mills, though generally the construction is lighter and, of course, the disposition of the spokes has to allow for the donkey to enter the wheel. Two wheels in Hampshire are notable in that they only have one set of spokes, whereas all the others have sets of spokes connecting both ends of the treads to the axle.

Very many donkey wheels must have been dismantled over the years, to make way for other machinery and buildings, and knowledge of those that survived had become almost extinguished by the time of the first World War, when they had ceased to be in regular use. H. W. Dickinson, the historian of London's water supply, was able to write in 1915: "Formerly numbers of tread-mills were to be found, but it is doubtful if there now exists in this country another besides the one at Carisbrooke Castle." A correspondent of *The Times* suggested in 1928 that a complete list of donkey wheels should be compiled, for he found that the statement made by Dickinson was still being widely accepted.

The challenge was taken up, consciously or not, by J. Steele Elliott, whose *Bygone Water Supplies*, published in 1933, records several donkey wheels. This article leans heavily on Steele Elliott. It also draws on my own research done in collaboration with Kenneth Major in spare moments over five years and published as a paper in the May 1972 issue of *Industrial Archaeology* under the title "*Water Raising by Animal Power*". The study owes a great deal to the readers of *Country Life* who responded most helpfully to a letter published in the journal on September 22, 1966. One reader, recalling holidays spent at East Hoe, Hambledon, Hampshire, in about 1902 wrote: "When we felt like it and to give the donkey a rest, my young brother and I used to do the donkey work which we much enjoyed."

Donkey wheels can be seen at Burton Agnes Old Hall, Yorkshire; Carisbrooke Castle, Isle of Wight; and Greys Court, Oxfordshire. They are also on display, having been removed from their original sites, at the museums of Maidstone, Kent; Luton, Bedfordshire; the Weald and Downland Open Air Museum, Singleton, Sussex; and the Lackham College of Agriculture, Lacock, Wiltshire.

It must be admitted that the treadwheel crane is something of a by-way in the history of technology. It is not a particularly economical means of generating power and does not lend itself for use by the larger animals like the horse and the ox. Wheels turned by animals in a horizontal plane are of much greater significance, for the great 18th-century engineers, such as John Smeaton, designed machines for powering by horses as readily as wind, water and steam-powered machines. Nevertheless, at their best these treadwheels are splendid products of the wheelwright's craft, with a continuous history of manufacture of some 2,000 years. There are now so few of them left that those few deserve protection.

Hugo Brunner
Country Life 1972

REALITY IN GRANADA

Plácido and Isabel were a young couple with four or five children who lived in great poverty. They owned a few strips of land and a small donkey with the aid of which Plácido used to supplement his peasant's earnings by collecting and selling brushwood. Then one day the donkey fell and broke its leg. This was a calamity, since they could not afford to buy another, and I went to see if I could help them over it.

I found Isabel, nursing a baby and surrounded by several grubby infants, on the verge of tears.

"There's nothing to be done," she said. "Nothing. We'll have to throw the donkey away. It goes to my heart, as it's been brought up with the children and is almost one of the family. Such a good little beast too – it has never been known to show the least malice. The tiniest of our children can play with it. I really think I mind it more on the *animalico's* account than on ours."

I asked her what she meant by saying that she would throw it away. "Oh, just that," she answered, and on being pressed explained that they would push it down a precipitous slope into the ravine where dead and dying animals were thrown. There it would lie with two or three legs broken till it died or the vultures finished it off.

"But how can you even think of such a thing?" I exclaimed. "Just imagine what it will suffer. You must kill it first."

"Oh, we could never do that," she replied. "Haven't I said that it has been brought up in our house among the family? Poor little animal, we could never treat it in that way."

And it turned out that no one in the village ever killed mules or donkeys or cows. Pigs were slaughtered and also kids and lambs, but other animals were either thrown down the ravine or tied to a post till they starved to death. Such was the custom, which was defended on the grounds that no one could kill animals that had been brought up in the house. In this predicament, for I am very fond of donkeys, I approached Federico the smith, and offered him a sum of money to kill it. As a rule gipsies are not squeamish about slaughtering animals and they willingly eat donkey's flesh, which after all is the chief constituent of Spanish sausages, but he felt that the opinion of the village would be against him if he accepted and therefore refused. All I could do was to make Plácido promise to push the donkey over a real precipice where it would be instantaneously killed, though whether he carried this out I doubt. Village customs had a way of imposing themselves.

Gerald Brenan
South from Granada 1957

THE DONKEY EXPENDABLE

In the early 1900's donkeys were being used extensively in North Western Australia, taking over from the bullock teams. Many stations also bred mules, importing jacks from Spain for this purpose. Spain of course has been famous for many hundreds of years for its quality horses, donkeys and mules. These jacks were put over blood mares to produce a very fine type of saddle mule and over heavy mares to produce draught animals.

On the other side of our vast island continent, in Queensland, donkeys were also being imported, again chiefly for the production of mules. Tall, chocolate brown donkey jacks were preferred for this purpose and were brought to Queensland from Rawalpindi. Many stations bred mules chiefly for stock work, right up to the second world war.

Even as late as 1935 donkey jacks were imported into Queensland for this purpose, this time from the U.S.A. Three huge jacks, each standing over 15 hands, were brought into the state to breed mules for use on the cane farms.

During the second world war, the Americans in Queensland used donkeys extensively as pack animals, selling them to local kids for 2s. apiece when they left – lucky kids!

One lesson at least can be learnt from this fragmented evidence: what a mistake it is for those who care for the donkey to despise the mule. It is the mule that, in so many cases, has led to the careful breeding and preservation of the donkey. Mules cannot be produced without a constant supply of donkey jacks – and donkey jacks cannot be bred without the jennies to bear them!

In countries where mules are not bred, such as Britain and Ireland, we find a deterioration of the donkey, a diminution in stature, a lack of speed and fire. In countries where mules are bred, and jacks with size, presence and "go" are required to breed good mules we find quality donkeys.

We hear about the donkeys being "turned loose" when no longer required as draught animals when motorised transport became general, but in actual fact, this term is not strictly true. They always were loose, the owners simply ceased to round them up as they had done at regular intervals before. In Western Australia unbranded animals of three years old or more become the property of the Crown. Similarly in the Northern Territory if the obvious owner cannot be found.

It seems a tragic reflection on Man and his sense of values that animals that were once so invaluable – who played such a vital part in the opening up of this great country – should, in a generation or two, be thought of as vermin and hunted down in their thousands to be killed for the bounty paid on their ears or as pets' meat.

Make no mistake about it. Donkeys *are* being slaughtered annually in

Working mules in Australia

their thousands. In Western Australia where the descendants of the once so highly prized donkey teams are declared vermin, they are hunted and shot – with the avowed aim of exterminating them. It is unlikely that this will happen because the donkey is intelligent, fleet of foot and living in a terrain that suits him perfectly.

The ancestors of these donkeys were yoked together in huge teams of over twenty donkeys. The leaders of the team were all important and selected for their intelligence. No bit was used on any animal but the whole team was controlled by verbal command. There are many men who will testify to the wonderful sagacity and willingness of these donkeys. They will tell you how when the donkey teams had their drays up to the axles in the sand of a dry river bed they would pull – and pull – till slowly, inch by inch, the load moved. A horse team would pull a few times then give up until the load was lightened or more horses brought in to add to the team.

In Western Australia, once the donkeys had been declared vermin, the station owners were bound to attempt to exterminate them. They must either arrange their own donkey shoots or pay levies so that professional shooters could be brought in to do the job. A bounty, usually ranging from 2s. 6d. – 7s. 6d. a pair of ears, was paid. At this price, donkey shooting was a lucrative profession! A journalist once told me that in the fifties he was in a small country town in Central Australia when a ute drove in, its stock rails so festooned with a macabre awning of donkeys' ears it was almost invisible.

The figures are astronomical: 1,000 donkeys shot in three weeks on one station, 888 shot by two men in two weeks, 10,000 donkeys in one year on one Northern Territory Station – 12,000 in a year on a West Australian station. Yet the donkey in Australia is not extinct.

But the commerically minded have seen another use for these "vermin". The vast open maw of the pet food market. Thousands of donkeys are slaughtered annually to supply this insatiable demand; some, it is rumoured, even to make salami. Some – the fortunate ones – have been slaughtered on their home territory as the mobile freezers have gone north. The less fortunate have been captured and trucked, or sent by train, vast distances under appalling conditions to the city abattoirs in the South and East.

For many years those who really have the welfare of animals at heart have been sickened by this trade and a few lone battlers have tried to do something about it; but unfortunately, in this world, the lone battler is seldom listened to, more often labelled "crank"!

Ann Walker
Australian Donkeys 1973

COMBINED OPERATIONS

One late afternoon in the high Sierra, a long line of burros was toiling up a rugged trail south of Mount Goddard. Each animal was loaded with heavy pack boxes covered with tarpaulins, so that the whole train, from a distance, looked like the crawling segments of a great snake. At the same time, in a small meadow some distance in front of the burros was a large flock of sheep and goats, tended by an aged Basque herder. He had with him several large sheepdogs, black and collie-like in appearance, but with the dispositions of wolves. They snapped and fought continually among themselves, but, for all that, served the shepherder well.

All was peace with the flock of sheep when the first of the string of burros scrabbled up over a ridge of Sierra granite and dropped down into the meadow. The dogs pricked up their ears, and two of them stopped a quarrel to look at the newcomers. Here was sport, indeed. Or perhaps they thought it was their duty to battle the invaders. It appeared to be pure mongrel viciousness to me, however, when two of the largest curs dashed toward the oncoming pack line with loud barks and snarls. The burros stopped for a moment as the dogs rushed toward them. Their long ears swung back and forth as though wondering what the dogs meant. Then they resumed their way, interested, but not in the least frightened, and making no detour around the dogs.

If there had been any doubt as to whether there would be a clash, this advance settled it. The larger of the two dogs wrinkled up his lips in a snarl that would have done credit to a hyena and rushed at the legs of the lead animal. A moment before, the burro had looked so much the plodding dullard that I thought surely he would be torn to pieces or, possibly, muster enough energy to flee. But no. The second that the dog hit his legs, the burro turned with lightning-like rapidity, despite the heavy pack, and kicked a slender hoof into the face of the snarling dog. At the same moment he opened his cavernous mouth and brayed with all the power of his lungs. It was not a bray of distress or of entreaty. It was defiant as a battle cry, and rang over the mountain slopes like a trumpet. I had never heard a burro bray like that before, and I never have since.

The second burro took up the cry; and the third, and the fourth. In a moment the battle shout spread down the line to the last burro, although half of them had not yet crossed the ridge, and could not see the dogs. Never had any of those dogs heard anything so awe-inspiring as fifty burros on the war-path, all braying at once. Indeed, we ourselves, who led the train, were startled, to say the least.

Whatever may be said of them, the sheepdogs were no cowards. After the din had subsided to some extent, they renewed their attack. The first burros crowded up into a line facing the dogs and all the burros in the rear broke into a run and came pouring down into the meadow like cavalry. Before the collies could realize what had happened, they were completely surrounded by a ring of pack beasts, long ears laid back and teeth showing. They were two surprised curs. Never in all their canine experience had any such calamity as this ever fallen upon them; and calamity it was to be in that circle of burro fury. One dog thought he saw an opening in the circle, and ran for it with his tail between his legs. The nearest burro quickly lowered his head. His teeth closed fairly over the dog's back. Even from where I was, I could hear the bones crunch and the cry of the beast as the burro threw up his head and tossed the limp body over his back outside the circle. Almost at the same time the other dog met a similar fate as he, too, made a dash for freedom. The sudden change of affairs had dampened the ardour of the two or three dogs which had thought to follow the first two. They were outside that dreaded circle and realized that that was the place to be. After the death of the second cur, three or four burros swelled out their nostrils and brayed loudly, as though the job were finished. Then all resumed their sleepy and plodding appearance and fell back into line. They were again "just burros".

Frank C. Hibben
Nature Magazine 1929

WILD ASSES IN SOMALIA

To any person who has only seen tame donkeys, even the beautiful ones of Upper Egypt and the Northern Sudan, the sight of a wild ass in movement across its native ground is a revelation. They are the poetry of motion! The ease and grace and swiftness with which they crossed or climbed or descended those terribly rough naked rocks, where we saw them, made the ibexes look like silly little jumping goats, and would have made a thoroughbred horse look like some rheumatic old screw. On the level plains, the Beni Amer told me, they are so swift and tireless that no mounted horse or racing camel can ever catch them.

The two jennies moved along a low ridge that ran across our front, halting for a while to look curiously at us, and Annette got a number of tele-photos before they dropped into a little Khor leading down to Wadi Sharag. When we returned to camp we saw them standing out on the sand in the open wadi, waiting to go back into Jebel Gadem.

Now, all this was intensely interesting for several reasons. Firstly, because their presence in this area was not known – at any rate to the Game Department: secondly because these animals have become so rare that, although they have been protected for years, they were thought to be almost extinct. Then they are of special interest because they are the ancestors of all the tame donkeys with which we are all familiar. But above all their beauty and grace of movement is so exquisite that all the superb deer, antelope, wild sheep and other animals I have known and admired seem stilted and stiff in comparison. I'd make an exception of the big cats. If one could cross a blood stallion with a female jaguar, one might get something that could compare with the Nubian wild ass.

. . . The general description of this rare and beautiful animal – perhaps by now (1958) exterminated – is a graceful and glorious beast such as I have described, about four feet (or twelve hands) tall at the withers: about the height of a Welsh mountain pony, or a little more. They are of golden fawn colour in the light of the sun and a rabbit-grey-fawn in shadow, exactly blending with their desert rocky background. They have a thin upstanding mane but no forelock at all. A strongly-marked chocolate dorsal stripe runs from mane to tail, crossed by a bold shoulder stripe which is conspicuous on either side. There are no barrings on the legs (these are the natural markings of the Somali wild ass: a different race). There is a white ring round the eye: and the underparts and lower parts of the legs are white.

Michael Mason
The Wild Ass Free 1959

THE ASS IN LEGEND

If a less elevated position in the hierarchy of mythology was reserved for the ass, it was because he seemed less useful and domesticated to the earliest inhabitants of Asia, where he lived running wild and free on the plains, beautifully formed, endowed with agility and elegance, fleet of foot and terrible of voice. And the terrifying power of his brays must have filled the hearts and minds of those early shepherds with a mysterious awe for them to have given the ass the name *gardabha* meaning "the resounding". For, while the fecund and gentle cow symbolizes a beneficent deity in Indian mythology, the onager, or wild ass, on the other hand, is more often than not a demon. He plays the role of the centaurs in Greek mythology, and of the ogres and monsters which romantic legends are full of. Indeed, the myths identify the *gardabha* with the *gandarvha*, the Indian centaur; and to this monster, half ass, half god, the vedic books which are the Bible of ancient India, attribute customs and actions which are certainly more frightening than reassuring. If there is a mythical treasure to guard, it is the Gandarvi who play the role of Cerberus; if a beautiful virgin smiles lovingly at impassioned shepherds, it is again the Gandarvi who, forgetting their nymphs the Apsare, fly upon the waters to seduce them with their cunning arts. The poet Atarvhaveda, the Veda of the domestic hearth, records one of their invocations: "Your wives are the Apsare, O Gandarvi, and you are their husbands. As you are immortal you should not run after mortal women." Oh yes! With characteristic pertinacity the Gandarvi pursue and seduce mortal girls. It is the eternal legend of love which was illustrated for the medieval populace by the devil who, taking the form of a handsome young man, seduced innocent maidens; a legend that has found its ultimate popular and artistic expression in the gloomy and sad story of Faust and Margherita. You might think that these celestial asses so indulgent with women elsewhere are equally so with their own. Quite the contrary! They are proudly jealous of them, and the least that they can do is to allow a little tolerated rival to become one of themselves. To be sure, if I may digress a little, it can never seem very dignified to become an ass through love; but it is nonetheless true that a large part of the literature of the ass refers to this unedifying metamorphosis. On the other hand, it seems to me that such fables illustrate the supreme moral concept – that voluptuousness transforms and bestializes man.

Guiseppe Finzi
L'Asino nella Leggenda
e la Letteratura 1883

A Persian miniature in the Topkapi Palace, Istanbul

The Duchess of Cleveland riding down Battle High Street

THE ESTEEMED WHITE ASS

The "white" riding-ass, now widely distributed throughout the Middle and Near East, and called here for brevity the Damascus Ass, was first bred in Syria . . . Very few specimens of this strain have been brought back from the Orient to England, but the giant white "Egyptian" Jack exhibited by the Prince of Wales, which won third prize at Islington Donkey Show in 1866, was certainly one of these, and twenty years later another super-ass from the same source was to be seen ridden in Battle and Hastings by none other than the Duchess of Cleveland, then occupant of Battle Abbey. This animal was about fourteen hands high; when it carried the Duchess it had a side-saddle, with snaffle bridle, but the manner in which Her Grace is seen in extant photographs, wielding the stick in the traditional Levantine manner, suggests that probably the bridle was more for decoration than for steering, and that direction was indicated as of old, by taps on the side of the neck. The latter ass was undoubtedly either descended from or included among those brought home by Lord Kitchener from Egypt (or according to another account from Palestine, which is equally possible), and presented to the Royal Family. The Duchess had been a bridesmaid at the wedding of Queen Victoria.

Anthony Dent
Donkey: The Story of the Ass
from East to West 1972

IN THE ARAN ISLANDS

Asses are numerous – practically every household owning one – and they are well treated. Between the intervals of drawing seaweed and turf, which are their principal jobs, they are turned loose amongst the sandhills where they fend for themselves. On asking a man who had some difficulty in catching his animal was he not rather a heavy burden for the beast he replied: "Sure if ye don't give him work he gets that lively there is no standing him".

On the occasion of my visit to Inishmaan my rest was very disturbed on the first two nights – dogs were barking and asses were galloping along the roads. It was at the time of year when the asses were free on the sandhills and during the night they quietly approached the gardens around the cottages where cabbages were grown. Listening carefully the ass would "nose" a loose stone from the top of the wall. If there was no response from the dogs he would gradually lower the wall until he could step over it into the garden, where he made a devastating meal. The dogs were not tied up and, to their credit, this seldom occurred – they were faithful guardians but the resulting noise of battle was like Bedlam let loose.

Not knowing the cause I made enquiries and, on receiving the information, remarked that I had no idea that asses could travel so fast as the noise of their hoofs seemed to indicate.

"Well," said my hostess, Mrs. Kate Flaherty (Roger), "do you not know that the ass travels best at night?"

I pleaded ignorance and asked the reason. The reply revealed a very beautiful tradition which I had not previously heard: "Sure, when the Holy Family were on the flight into Egypt they travelled with an ass by night and rested during the day, and ever since the ass travels best at night"

Thomas H. Mason
The Islands of Ireland 1967

AN ERROR OF JUDGEMENT

"Many's the night I was in and out of those attics, following my poor uncle when he had a bad turn on him – the horrors, y'know – there were nights he never stopped walking through the house. Good Lord! will I ever forget the morning he said he saw the devil coming up the avenue. 'Look at the two horns on him,' says he, and he out with his gun and shot him, and, begad, it was his own donkey!"

E. OE. Somerville & Martin Ross
The Irish R.M. and His Experiences 1899

3. Donkeys Delectable

TO A YOUNG ASS, ITS MOTHER BEING TETHERED NEAR IT

Poor little foal of an oppressed race!
I love the languid patience of thy face:
And oft with gentle hand I give thee bread,
And clap thy ragged coat, and pat thy head.
But what thy dullèd spirits hath dismay'd,
That never thou dost sport along the glade?
And (most unlike the nature of things young)
That earthward still thy moveless head is hung?
Do thy prophetic fears anticipate,
Meek child of misery! thy future fate?
The starving meal, and all the thousand aches
"Which patient merit of the unworthy takes"?
Or is thy sad heart thrill'd with filial pain
To see thy wretched mother's shortened chain?
And truly, very piteous is *her* lot –
Chained to a log within a narrow spot
Where the close-eaten grass is scarcely seen,
While sweet around her waves the tempting green.
Poor ass! thy master should have learnt to show
Pity – best taught by fellowship of woe!
For much I fear me that *he* lives like thee,
Half famished in a land of luxury!
How *askingly* its footsteps hither bend?
It seems to say, "And have I then *one* friend?"
Innocent foal! thou poor despised forlorn!
I hail thee brother – spite of the fool's scorn!
And fain would take thee with me, in the dell
Of peace and mild equality to dwell,
Where Toil shall call the charmer Health his bride,
And Laughter tickle Plenty's ribless side!
How thou wouldst toss thy heels in gamesome play,
And frisk about, as lamb or kitten gay!
Yea! and more musically sweet to me
Thy dissonant harsh bray of joy would be,
Than warbled melodies that soothe to rest
The aching of pale Fashion's vacant breast!

Samuel Taylor Coleridge *1794*

'Rushlake Renata', two days old

THE DONKEY

I saw a donkey
    One day old,
His head was too big
    For his neck to hold;
His legs were shaky
    And long and loose,
They rocked and staggered
    And weren't much use.
He tried to gambol
    And frisk a bit,
But he wasn't quite sure
    Of the trick of it.
His queer little coat
    Was soft and grey
And curled at his neck
    In a lovely way.
His face was wistful
    And left no doubt
That he felt life needed
    Some thinking out.
So he blundered round
    In venturous quest,
And then lay flat
    On the ground to rest.
He looked so little
    And weak and slim,
I prayed the world
    Might be good to him.

Gertrude Hind *Punch 1928*

DAPPLE STOLEN

But destiny, which, according to the opinion of those who have not the light of the true faith, guides and disposes all things in its own way, so ordered it, that Gines de Passamonte, the famous cheat and robber (whom the valour and phrenzy of Don Quixote had delivered from the chain), being justly afraid of the holy brotherhood, took it into his head to hide himself among those very mountains; and in the very place where, by the same impulse, Don Quixote and Sancho Panza had taken refuge; arriving just in time to distinguish who they were, although they had fallen asleep. Now, as the wicked are always ungrateful, and necessity urges desperate measures, and present convenience over-balances every consideration of the future, Gines, who had neither gratitude nor good-nature, resolved to steal Sancho Panza's ass; not caring for Rozinante, as a thing neither pawnable nor saleable. Sancho Panza slept; the varlet stole his ass; and before dawn of day was too far off to be recovered.

Aurora issued forth, giving joy to the earth, but grief to Sancho Panza,

who, when he missed his Dapple, began to utter the most doleful lamentations, insomuch that Don Quixote awaked at his cries and heard him say: "O child of my bowels, born in my house, the joy of my children, the entertainment of my wife, the envy of my neighbours, the relief of my burdens, and lastly, the half of my maintenance! – for with the six and twenty maravedis which I have earned every day by thy means, have I half supported my family!" Don Quixote, on learning the cause of these lamentations, comforted Sancho in the best manner he could, and desired him to have patience, promising to give him a bill of exchange for three asses out of five which he had left at home. Sancho, comforted by this promise, wiped away his tears, moderated his sighs, and thanked his master for the kindness he showed him. . . .

At this time they saw a man coming towards them mounted upon an ass, and as he drew near he had the appearance of a gypsy. But Sancho Panza, who, whenever he saw an ass, followed it with eyes and heart, had no sooner got a glimpse of the man, than he recognized Gines de Passamonte, and, by the same clue, was directed to his lost ass; it being really Dapple himself on which Gines was mounted! for in order to escape discovery and sell the animal, he had disguised himself like a gypsy, as he could speak their language, among many others, as readily as his native tongue.

Sancho immediately called out aloud to him, "Ah, rogue Ginesillo! leave my darling, let go my life, rob me not of my comfort, quit my sweetheart, leave my delight; – fly, rapscallion – fly! get you gone, thief! and give up what is not your own."

So much railing was not necessary; for at the first word Gines dismounted in a trice, and taking to his heels was out of sight in an instant. Sancho ran to his Dapple, and, embracing him, said: "How hast thou done, my dearest Dapple, delight of my eyes, my sweet companion!"

Then he kissed and caressed him as if he had been a human creature. The ass held his peace and suffered himself to be thus kissed and caressed by Sancho, without answering him one word. They all came up and wished him joy on the restoration of his Dapple; especially Don Quixote, who at the same time assured him that he should not on that account revoke his order for the three colts; for which he had Sancho's hearty thanks.

Miguel de Cervantes
Don Quixote 1605

Gines with Sancho Panza's 'Dapple'

DAPPLE AT THE CASTLE

Sancho was overjoyed to find himself so much in the Duchess's favour . . . so transported, that he even forsook his beloved Dapple to keep close to the Duchess, and entered the castle with the company; but his conscience flying in his face for leaving that dear companion of his alone, he went to a reverend old waiting-woman, who was one of the Duchess's retinue, and whispering in her ear, "Mrs. Gonzales, or Mrs. – pray forsooth may I crave your name?" "Donna Rodriguez de Grijalva is my name", said the old duenna; "what is your business with me, friend?" "Pray now, mistress", quoth Sancho, "do so much as go out of the castle gate, where you will find a dapple ass of mine; see him into the stable or else put him in yourself; for, poor thing, it is main fearful and timorsome, and cannot abide to be alone in a strange place". "If the master", said she pettishly, "has no more manners than the man, we shall have a fine time of it. Get you gone, you saucy jack, the Devil take thee and him that brought you hither to affront me. Go seek somewhere else for ladies to look to your ass, you lolpoop! I would have you know that gentlewomen like me are not used to such drudgeries". "Do not take pepper in your nose at it", replied Sancho, "you need not be so frumpish, mistress. As good as you have done it. I have heard my master say (and he knows all the histories in the world) that when Sir Lancelot came out of Britain, damsels looked after him and waiting-women after his horse. Now, by my troth! whether you believe it or not, I would not swop my ass for Sir Lancelot's horse, I will tell you that". "I think the fool rides the fellow", quoth the waiting-woman; "hark you, fellow, if you be a buffoon, keep your stuff for those chapmen that will bid you fairer. I would not give a fig for all the jests in your budget". "Well enough yet", quoth Sancho, "and a fig for you too, if you go to that. Adad! should I take thee for a fig, I might be sure of a ripe one, your fig is rotten ripe, forsooth; say no more: if sixty is the game, you are a peep-out". "You rascally son of a whore", cried the waiting-woman, in a pelting chafe, "whether I am old or not, Heaven best knows, I shall not stand to give an answer to such a ragamuffin as thou garlic-eating stinkard". She spoke this so loud that the Duchess overheard her; and seeing the woman so altered, and as red as fire, asked what was the matter. "Why, madam," said the waiting-woman, "here is a fellow would have me put his ass in the stable: telling me an idle story of ladies that looked after one Lancelot, and waiting-women after his horse; and because I will not be his ostler, the rake-shame very civilly calls me old". "Old?" said the Duchess, "that is an affront no woman can bear well. You are mistaken, honest Sancho, Rodriguez is very young, and the long veil she wears is more for authority and fashion-sake than upon account of her years". "May there be never a good one in all those days I have to live", quoth Sancho, "if I meant her any harm, only I have such a natural love for my ass, if it like your worship, that I thought I could not recommend the poor tilt to a more charitable body than this same Madam Rodriguez". "Sancho", said Don Quixote, with a sour look, "does this talk befit this place? Do you know where you are?" "Sir", quoth Sancho, "every man must tell his wants, be he where he will. Here I bethought myself of Dapple, and here I spoke of him: had I called him to mind in the stable, I would have spoken of him there".

"Sancho has reason on his side" said the Duke; "and nobody ought to chide him for it. But let him take no further care, Dapple shall have as much provender as he will eat, and be used as well as Sancho himself."

Miguel de Cervantes
Don Quixote 1605

An ass laden with gold climbs to the top of the castle.

Thomas Fuller
Gnomologia: Adagies and Proverbs 1732

DONEGAL

Donegal is surely the most enchanting place in Ireland . . . hills come out of the mist and stand up boldly blue as the sea: a lark takes to the sky, a plover wheels and cries above the green bogland; the little oddly-shaped walls shine out on the blue hills; white cabins shine; a girl with a shawl over her head comes along the road driving a donkey; and there is something in all this like a fairy-tale. You look at her, half expecting that she will come and tell you that she is a princess in disguise; half-expecting that the poor moth-eaten little beast will lift an eye to you and indicate in some dumb way that he, poor fellow, is searching for the enchanted rose.

The light that turns Donegal into a poem for an hour, or for only a second, is a terrible and disturbing thing. If any man with a sense of beauty were compelled to see it every day it would unfit him for the practical business of life. I think that if ever Ireland produces a Joan of Arc the angel will come to her as she is driving an old grey donkey down the road in Donegal after the lifting of a storm.

H. V. Morton
In Search of Ireland 1930

DONKEY DIVERSIONS

If we may believe what John Leo tells us in his description of Egypt, the ass would not seem to be so stupid and indocile an animal as he is commonly represented.

"When the Mahometan sermons and worship are over, the common people of Cairo resort to the part of suburbs called Bed Ellogh, as well as the stage-players, and those who teach camels, asses and dogs to dance. The dancing of the ass is diverting enough, for after he has frisked and capered about, his master tells him that the Soldan meaning to build a great palace, intends to employ all the asses in carrying mortar, stones and other materials; upon which the ass falls down with his heels upwards, closing his eyes as if he were dead.

This done the master begs some assistance of the company, to make up for the loss of the dead ass; and having collected all he can get, gives them to know that truly his ass is not really dead but only being sensible of his master's necessity, played that trick to procure some provender. Then he commands the ass to rise, who still lies in the same position, notwithstanding all the blows he can give him; till at least he proclaims, that by virtue of an edict by the Soldan, all the handsome ladies are bound to ride out next day upon the comeliest asses they can find, in order to see a triumphal show; and to entertain their asses with oats and Nile water.

No sooner are these words spoken than the ass starts up, and prances and leaps for joy. But the master instantly gives out that his ass was pitched upon by the warden of his street, to carry his deformed and ugly wife; upon which the ass lowers his ears and limps with one of his legs as if he were lame. Then the master alleging that his ass has kindness for handsome women, commands him to single out the prettiest lady in the company, and accordingly he makes his choice by going round and touching one of the prettiest with his head; upon which, the company divert themselves by laughing and pointing to the ass's 'sweetheart' ".

From: *Harris's Collection of Voyages*
The Sporting Magazine 1806

DORCAS

To describe Dorcas, one must describe her twice. Because the ass I play with all summer is hardly to be recognised as the one that is the unofficial mascot of the local Modern School through two winter terms.

Although the summer is nearly over before the last tassel of winter coat falls away, she is in the warm months a sleek creature, suggesting seal-black hind quarters that fade attractively into grey shoulders and legs. If her rump is looked at closely it will be seen to have only the *appearance* of black, being in fact a mixture of black hairs with white. The inner parts of her hind legs and her stomach are white, the belly-hair long and very soft. Her neck and stubby head are grey, with a white line running like a broad hat elastic under her throat, and she never entirely loses the year round the chunks of thick hair on her cheeks which give her a Gladstonian air. The wide brow is white, and in the summer twilight it glimmers ghostlike far down the field when the rest of her has blended with the night shadows. Her nose too is white, shading down to pale grey between the nostrils; and all around her mouth and this lower part of her nose, which is softer to the fingers than finest suede, is protected by a nimbus of long whiskers. These are plentiful, but so fine that the unobservant eye may miss them.

Her ears, most expressive of her features, are brownish, and from the insides hang protective butter-coloured fringes. (Lucky for her that she did not live a hundred years earlier or those lengthy ears might have been docked to the size of a horse's, for the greater convenience of putting on and off her collar.)

Dorcas's eyelashes, white as an ancient man's, thick as an actress's, fringe eyes that are large and liquid, dark blue in the iris depths. Beneath each eye is a sparse line of black hairs, each three to five inches in length: this strange adornment is so unobtrusive that it is likely many donkey-owners have not noticed it. Dorcas is shortsighted in that she does not recognize her friends at a middling distance; on the other hand she can see men, cows, machines, in distant fields, and often watches their movements for minutes at a time. Her hearing is as good as a dog's.

She does not have on her legs ugly "chestnuts" (castors, to give them their proper name), as a horse does. One of the less obvious differences between an ass and a horse is that the former never has castors on the hind legs. And those on the inside of Dorcas's forelegs, instead of being knobbly and wartlike, are flat, smooth, feeling and looking like black kid.

There are other interesting dissimilarities between horse and ass. The male ass has rudimentary teats, which the horse has not. Horses have a hard protective skin over the rump; in the ass this extends much further, covering the ribs. Hence has risen the mistaken belief, cause of so much cruelty, that a donkey can scarcely feel the hardest whacking. Not so long ago costermongers cut away a piece of the skin of the rump, to expose a raw and tender area for the lash. Less drastic, but equally if not more injurious, is the still prevalent habit of kicking a donkey in the stomach. Yet even a gentle tap with a leafy twig will make Dorcas hasten her steps.

There is a difference, too, in the formation of the feet, or hoofs, of a horse and an ass. But this is not obvious, and certainly does *not* extend to clovenfootedness! It would seem as foolishly unnecessary to mention this as to remark that a stag bears antlers, were it not for the fact that on several Christmas and birthday cards of the more frivolous type, donkeys are depicted with feet cloven as a pig's.

Everyone knows, of course, the difference in tails; the ass's not being a complete plume of hair, but starting off for the first few inches like a cow's.

The cow has a comparatively short tassel at the end of a long smooth tail; and though the donkey's is often described as cowlike, in fact the smooth part is very short indeed. Dorcas's tail, after combing, comes from its tangle into a plentiful tassel, and can be seen to be made up of hairs of three distinct colours: black, brown, white; the overall effect being brownish, like her ears. Her mane is not one to be proud of, and insists on falling skimpily half on one side of her neck, half on the other. Donkeys never have the luxurious growth that adorns the necks of horses. Or rarely. The fine, tall asses from Poitou, in France, used for mule-breeding, have hanging, horselike manes.

In September, Dorcas's hair begins to grow again, and by the time cold weather comes she is well clad for it in her thick, very shaggy, brownish coat of exactly the shade that the fashion-writers call "donkey". They could as well have chosen another shade. Donkeys vary through all the greys and browns, including chocolate and a lovely honey colour. The chocolate-brown

ones are often beautifully marked, with cream noses and cream circles round their eyes, the very hues of a Siamese cat. There are white donkeys, too, but these are quite a rarity in England. In biblical times they were chosen as the mounts of kings and leaders.

By Christmas Dorcas's brow has grown a polar-shaggy silver fringe to shield her eyes from cold winds and rain. Her almost yaklike coat now makes her look smaller than her ten and a half hands, as though she were weighted down by the heaviness of it.

The crowning beauty of the ass is the mark of the Cross upon his back, laid there, legend says, since the day that Christ rode into Jerusalem and the palms were strewn before Him.

Dorcas, alas! bears no Cross, and that is the only thing about her that disappoints me. For donkeys, through symbol, through tradition, are holy beasts, and ought to carry the Sign. Were they not in the Stable, too, when Christ was born?

As a country man said to me, searching for words, not articulate:

"I've always liked donkeys, from the Bible and that, and our Lord riding one. I think if you've got any bottom to you at all you like them; for they're the bottom of everything."

This may not be very clear, but only the too sophisticated will not know exactly what he meant.

And, indeed, one of the more surprising things about ownership of Dorcas is the number of people who are enchanted by her – and I stress that she is not, as donkeys go, a comely ass. Perhaps in some deep, unconscious layer of their minds these people, many of them urban in life and thought, are recognizing what my country friend was trying to put into words.... Anyway, as I lead her down the road, cars slow up, heads strain out, voices exclaim, pedestrians stop and speak. So many say, wistfully, "I've always thought I'd like to have a donkey."

Doris Rybot
My Kingdom for a Donkey 1963

FRANCESCA AND MIRANDA

Miranda has been with me now for nine years. Francesca for six. As they did not bring any birth certificates with them, I cannot swear to their precise ages. Both were sold to me as three-year-olds, so by now Miranda should be twelve and Francesca nine; and a little while ago, when I asked the local vet how old he thought they were, his estimate just about coincided with my calculations.

Miranda derives her name from the fact that she arrived in a tempest – actually a heavy snowstorm. When it came to Francesca's turn we could not think of any Shakespearean heroine with whom she could also be linked, so in the end she was called after myself, my middle name being Frances.

Why did I choose donkeys as pets? Well, I wanted to have some animal of my own in addition to the foxes, deer and squirrels who are regular visitors, and the bats and the bees who are – not altogether welcome and certainly uninvited – residents under my roof. But I live a very full and complicated life, and a dog or a cat would need more attention than I can be sure of giving them; and it is always a problem to know what to do with house pets when one goes away. Donkeys, I thought, would be reasonably self-sufficient: also, if I could get fairly young ones there was a good prospect that they would outlive me, and I should be able to enjoy them to the end of my days. And to clinch the matter, my neighbour who owns a large meadow adjoining my garden, expressed his willingness to give them hospitality in return for whatever they could do to keep the grass under control.

Before Francesca arrived, Miranda had first an elderly mare, and subsequently a retired piebald circus pony, to keep her company, neither of which belonged to me. She is not at all fussy about whom she lives with, and was inseparable from each of these companions in turn as she now is from Francesca. Moreover her affection appears to have been reciprocated at least by Penny, the circus pony. After his owner removed him to a field about a mile away, he continually broke out and galloped across my garden in order to talk to Miranda over the fence. Eventually I had to erect a barrier to save my garden even at the expense of the lovers.

Miranda is a highly disciplined, uncomplaining character. As long as Penny was around she used occasionally to indulge in whole-hearted braying. (Don't believe it if anyone tells you that female donkeys don't bray. Both mine disprove it.) Since Penny left – six years ago – she has never uttered, though whether there is any connection between these facts I do not know. Anyhow, I always think of Miranda, who is of classical donkey appearance, grey with a white underbelly and a well marked cross on her back, as a pillar of the Establishment. She always conducts herself with dignity and decorum, and would never fawn upon you in the hope of getting a carrot or a peppermint; nor, I am sure, would she ever man the barricades or rebel against legitimate authority.

Not so Francesca. Francesca has a dark brown shaggy coat and an untidy fringe falls over her face. Her woolly legs always remind me of the thick black stockings that were so popular with Chelsea girls a year or two ago. Whenever she sees a likely giver of titbits, she starts to whimper pathetically, and she never hesitates to raise her voice if anything – the weather for instance – is not to her liking. One day last winter I was to make a recording for the B.B.C. and the producer said that he would prefer to do this at my home rather than in Broadcasting House, so as to "get more atmosphere". It so happened that this resulted in the donkeys' evening feed being delayed for half an hour or so. Miranda, of course, kept a stiff upper lip, but Francesca gave voice to loud and frequent protests, all of which inevitably found their way on to the tape. So when the record went on the air, it had to be preceded by an explanation of the background noises. Maybe the producer got more atmosphere than he bargained for!

Most people, I notice, who talk about their donkeys say what affectionate pets they make. I could not, however, honestly say that either of mine shows much evidence (other than cupboard love) of affection for humans. Whether this is due to unfortunate infantile experiences about which I know nothing, or to the fact that I have not been able to talk to them and play with them as much as I could wish, is anybody's guess; but the fact is that nine times out of ten (the tenth time they relent) if you try to fondle them, they disengage themselves much in the way that children do when they are irritated by the attentions of an unwelcome adult.

But that is not to say that either Miranda or Francesca shows hostility or aggression towards man or beast: indeed I have seen Miranda playing happily with a dog, and even once with a rabbit; and once when they were both chased by an enormous horse, who was a temporary visitor, they won his abject devotion within 24 hours. Different as they are in so many ways, they are both alike in their imperturbably peaceable natures. I often think that, if some of our statesmen would model themselves upon Miranda or Francesca, the world would be a much happier place.

The Baroness Wootton of Abinger *1968*

PACIFICO THE CADDY

I am ten years old, small, dark brown in colour and I have often heard people say that I am very good looking. My name is Pacifico and I am a Jack-donkey.

Until one day in late December 1968, I lived with a charming and very kind Portuguese peasant in the Monchique hills, several hundred feet above sea level, in the province of Algarve in Southern Portugal.

My master loved me and was very patient, which accounts for my sweet and gentle disposition (I never kick or get nasty) and goes to prove that much can be achieved through kindness with my fellows of the animal world. In my former life I had no name but because of my exceptional temperament my new master called me Pacifico which means "tame" in Portuguese.

My life has undergone a tremendous change in the past eleven months. Before, when I lived in the hills, I was happy but worked very hard as my master was paralysed on one side of his body and I had to carry him and his goods up and down the mountain road, nearly always accompanied by the two rams who lived with me. We were very poor and could not afford all the proper kind of food we needed.

Well, these English people were lunching up in the hills one fine day in December, as I said before. They watched me amble up the road and for some reason best known to themselves decided that they would like me to go and live with them down in the plain near the sea, at a place called Penina. My Portugese master was most reluctant to part with me – we had been together since I was very young. However, after a long discussion an agreement was reached and two days later I was transferred by lorry to my new home.

This place, Penina, is something called a residential estate, in parkland, and a vast amount of lush, green grass grows on the part of it that is called a golf course. I share stables with four equines; two beautiful horses and a temperamental mare, who is my great friend, and a mule. We are extremely comfortable and enjoy very good food and regular grooming which is why I look so handsome these days.

Of course I still work, but it is of a different kind and most interesting to me. My new master, who has something to do with this golf course place, is known as Senhor Cotton and appears to be some kind of authority on the game of golf which he has trained me to follow. I usually walk round with him when he plays and carry two bags of clubs, one on each side of my saddle. When I do this, which I enjoy, they call me a caddy. Manuel, who is a young boy and wears a bright yellow uniform is also a caddy – all very confusing for those of you who may not know much about this strange game.

Henry Cotton with his caddy 'Pacifico'

Anyway, Manuel always comes round with me, fetches me from the stables, brushes me before I start work, and when we are not needed on the golf course trots me round the perimeter road of the estate, which is a good long outing. Manuel has a young donkey of his own, so we understand each other very well.

I enjoy caddying best though, especially as I have learned to stop walking when people do, which is super because it gives me many opportunities to nibble at that lush grass I was telling you about. There are places called tees where the players stop to put little hard round white things on even smaller little coloured wooden peg things and then hit the white thing – if you follow me. Well, on these tee places there are green cans filled with water, which I drink when I get thirsty. I know the cans are not put there especially for my convenience, but no one seems to mind.

As I said, I enjoy the work very much and have learnt quite a bit about the game so that when people play well I find it interesting and am quiet, and not critical – when play is bad I get bored and say so in no uncertain terms. Players think my braying means I am hungry and want to return to the stables, so they try to get a move on and usually my tactics work.

When I feel particularly happy I become mischievous and playful, very gently nipping my master or Manuel, nuzzling an arm or searching a pocket if I get a sniff of dried figs or, better still, apple or pear. Pear is a great treat which comes my way only occasionally – but I get a breakfast roll every day when I call at the club or am going round with Senhor Cotton, and never a day goes by without my ration of one beautiful, tasty, crunchy polo-mint.

I have had two complete new sets of shoes since I came to Penina and my coat was clipped in the Spring. My former master often enquires about me. He is always assured with complete truth that I love my new way of life. Who among us donkeys would not?

My story and photograph have appeared in many publications all over the world – only the other day some visiting travel agents from South America wanted to meet me, having read about me in their papers.

You could say that mine is the Cinderella story of the donkey world, if you know what I mean.

Dictated but not signed by PACIFICO,
Henry Cotton's Donkey 1970

DALMATIAN DONKEYS

Like dancers through the dawn they go
Tip-tapping, lightly shod,
Where pomegranates burnished glow
Against a golden road:
Picking their way fastidious, slow
Swinging their motley load.

Along the shore, beneath the pine
Or olive's silver shade;
They carry honey, fruit and wine,
A tinkling cavalcade
Passing in never-ending line
From decade to decade.

Turk or Spaniard, Roman, Greek,
Venetian argosies;
Though tyrants shatter, battles shake
The isle-infested seas,
Yet still the little donkeys seek
Their burden of all these.

Softly the Adriatic wakes
Dubrovnik from her dreams:
In opal splendour daylight breaks,
The sun-girt city gleams.
By rose-washed walls, past ancient gates
The strange procession streams.

Bearing the perfumed nectarine
Still fragrant from the sun,
Green fig and purple aubergine.
Against the heat-soaked stone
Tall, white-robed peasant women lean,
A frieze from Macedon.

As in a mounting ecstasy
Shimmering hangs the day;
Yet bearing still their argosy
The little donkeys sway.
Poor Brother Ass who endlessly
Pursues his patient way.

None think upon their lowly state
Continuing evermore,
The faint, grey shapes that ever wait
By Adriatic shore;
To pity them their humble fate
Who once a Saviour bore.

Joan Warburg

NICHOLAS NYE

Thistle and darnel and dock grew there,
    And a bush, in the corner, of may,
On the orchard wall I used to sprawl
    In the blazing heat of the day;
Half asleep and half awake,
    While the birds went twittering by,
And nobody there my lone to share
    But Nicholas Nye.

Nicholas Nye was lean and grey,
    Lame of a leg and old,
More than a score of donkey's years
    He had seen since he was foaled;
He munched the thistles, purple and spiked,
    Would sometimes stoop and sigh,
And turn his head, as if he said,
    'Poor Nicholas Nye!'

Alone with his shadow he'd drowse in the meadow,
    Lazily swinging his tail,
At break of day he used to bray,
    Not much too hearty and hale;
But a wonderful gumption was under his skin,
    And a clear calm light in his eye,
And once in a while he'd smile . . .
    Would Nicholas Nye.

Seem to be smiling at me, he would,
    From his bush in the corner, of may, –
Bony and ownerless, widowed and worn,
    Knobble-kneed, lonely and grey;
And over the grass would seem to pass,
    'Neath the deep dark blue of the sky,
Something much better than words between me
    And Nicholas Nye.

But dusk would come in the apple boughs,
    The green of the glow-worm shine,
The birds in nest would crouch to rest,
    And home I'd trudge to mine;
And there, in the moonlight, dark with dew,
    Asking not wherefore nor why,
Would brood like a ghost, as still as a post.
    Old Nicholas Nye.

Walter De La Mare *1913*

'Head of a Donkey' by James Ward R.A. 1769–1859

EEYORE LOSES A TAIL

The Old Grey Donkey, Eeyore, stood by himself in a thistly corner of the forest, his front feet well apart, his head on one side, and thought about things. Sometimes he thought sadly to himself, "Why?" and sometimes he thought, "Wherefore" and sometimes he thought "Inasmuch as which?" – and sometimes he didn't quite know what he *was* thinking about. So when Winnie-the-Pooh came stumping along, Eeyore was very glad to be able to stop thinking for a little, in order to say "How do you do?" in a gloomy manner to him.

"And how are you?" said Winnie-the-Pooh.

Eeyore shook his head from side to side.

"Not very how," he said. "I don't seem to have felt at all how for a long time".

"Dear, dear," said Pooh, "I'm sorry about that. Let's have a look at you."

So Eeyore stood there, gazing sadly at the ground, and Winnie-the-Pooh walked all round him once.

"Why, what's happened to your tail?" he said, in surprise.

"What has happened to it?" said Eeyore.

"It isn't there!"

"Are you sure?"

"Well, either a tail *is* there or it isn't there. You can't make a mistake about it. And yours *isn't* there!"

"Then what is?"

"Nothing."

"Let's have a look", said Eeyore, and he turned slowly round to the place where his tail had been a little while ago, and then, finding that he couldn't catch it up, he turned round the other way until he came back to where he was at first, and then he put his head down and looked between his front legs, and at last he said, with a long, sad sigh, "I believe you're right."

"Of course I'm right," said Pooh.

"That accounts for a Good Deal," said Eeyore gloomily. "It Explains Everything. No Wonder."

"You must have left it somewhere," said Winnie-the-Pooh.

"Somebody must have taken it," said Eeyore.

"How Like Them," he added, after a long silence.

Pooh felt that he ought to say something helpful about it, but didn't quite know what. So he decided to do something helpful instead.

"Eeyore," he said solemnly, "I, Winnie-the-Pooh, will find your tail for you."

"Thank you, Pooh," answered Eeyore. "You're a real friend," said he "Not like Some," he said.

So Winnie-the-Pooh went off to find Eeyore's tail.

It was a fine spring morning in the forest as he started out. Little soft clouds played happily in a blue sky, skipping from time to time in front of the sun as if they had come to put it out, and then sliding away suddenly so that the next might have his turn. Through them and between them the sun shone bravely; and a copse which had worn its firs all the year seemed old and dowdy now beside the new green lace which the beeches had put on so prettily. Through copse and spinney marched Bear; down open slopes of gorse and heather, over rocky beds of streams, up steep banks of sandstone into the heather again, and so at last, tired and hungry, to the Hundred Acre Wood. For it was in the Hundred Acre Wood that Owl lived.

"And if anyone knows anything about anything", said Bear to himself, "it's Owl who knows something about something", he said, "or my name's not Winnie-the-Pooh", he said. "Which it is", he added. "So there you are".

Owl lived at The Chestnuts, an old-world residence of great charm, which was grander than anybody else's, or seemed so to Bear, because it had both a knocker *and* a bell-pull. Underneath the knocker there was a notice which said:

PLES RING IF AN RNSER IS REQIRD.

Underneath the bell-pull there was a notice which said:

PLES CNOKE IF AN RNSR IS NOT REQID.

These notices had been written by Christopher Robin, who was the only one in the forest who could spell; for Owl, wise though he was in many ways, able to read and write and spell his own name WOL, yet somehow went all to pieces over delicate words like MEASLES and BUTTEREDTOAST.

Winnie-the-Pooh read the two notices very carefully, first from left to right, and afterwards, in case he had missed some of it, from right to left. Then, to make quite sure, he knocked and pulled the knocker, and he pulled and knocked the bell-rope, and he called out in a very loud voice, "Owl! I require an answer! It's Bear speaking". And the door opened and Owl looked out.

"Hallo, Pooh", he said. "How's things?"

"Terrible and sad", said Pooh, "because Eeyore, who is a friend of mine, has lost his tail. And he's Moping about it. So could you very kindly tell me how to find it for him?"

"Well", said Owl, "the customary procedure in such cases is as follows".

"What does Crustimony Proseedcake mean?" said Pooh. "For I am a Bear of very little Brain, and long words Bother me".

"It means the Thing to Do".

"As long as it means that, I don't mind", said Pooh humbly.

"The thing to do is as follows. First, Issue a Reward. Then – "

"Just a moment", said Pooh, holding up his paw. "*What* do we do to this – what you were saying? You sneezed just as you were going to tell me".

"I *didn't* sneeze.

"Yes, you did, Owl".

"Excuse me, Pooh, I didn't. You can't sneeze without knowing it".

"Well, you can't know it without something having been sneezed".

"What I *said* was, 'First *Issue* a Reward'."

"You're doing it again", said Pooh sadly.

"A Reward!" said Owl very loudly. "We write a notice to say that we will give a large something to anybody who finds Eeyore's tail".

"I see, I see", said Pooh, nodding his head. "Talking about large somethings", he went on dreamily, "I generally have a small something about now – about this time in the morning", and he looked wistfully at the cupboard in the corner of Owl's parlour; "just a mouthful of condensed milk or whatnot, with perhaps a lick of honey – "

"Well, then," said Owl, "we write out this notice and we put it up all over the Forest".

"A lick of honey", murmured Bear to himself, "or – or not, as the case may be". And he gave a deep sigh and tried very hard to listen to what Owl was saying.

But Owl went on and on, using longer and longer words, until at last he came back to where he started, and he explained that the person to write out this notice was Christopher Robin.

"It was he who wrote the ones on my front door for me. Did you see them, Pooh?"

For some time now Pooh had been saying "Yes" and "No" in turn, with his eyes shut, to all that Owl was saying, and having said "Yes, yes" last time, he said "No, not at all" now, without really knowing what Owl was talking about.

"Didn't you see them?" said Owl, a little surprised. "Come and look at them now".

So they went outside. And Pooh looked at the knocker and the notice below it, and he looked at the bell-rope and the notice below it, and the more he looked at the bell-rope, the more he felt that he had seen something like it somewhere else, sometime before.

"Handsome bell-rope, isn't it?" said Owl.

Pooh nodded.

"It reminds me of something", he said, "but I can't think what. Where did you get it?"

"I just came across it in the Forest. It was hanging over a bush, and I thought at first somebody lived there, so I rang it, and nothing happened, and then I rang it again very loudly and it came off in my hand, and as nobody seemed to want it, I took it home, and – ".

"Owl", said Pooh solemnly, "you made a mistake. Somebody did want it".

"Who?"

"Eeyore. My dear friend Eeyore. He was – he was fond of it".

"Fond of it?"

"Attached to it", said Winnie-the-Pooh sadly.

So with these words he unhooked it, and carried it back to Eeyore; and when Christopher Robin had nailed it on in its right place again, Eeyore frisked about the forest, waving his tail so happily that Winnie-the-Pooh came over all funny, and had to hurry home for a little snack of something to sustain him. And, wiping his mouth half an hour afterwards, he sang to himself proudly:

Who found the Tail?
"I", said Pooh,
"At a quarter to two
(Only it was quarter to eleven really).
I found the Tail!"

A. A. Milne
Winnie the Pooh 1926

A FAIRY TALE

Once upon a time there lived a King and a Queen, who were rich and had everything they wanted, but no children. The Queen lamented over this day and night, and said: "I am like a field on which nothing grows." At last God gave her her wish, but when the child came into the world, it did not look like a human child, but was a little donkey. When the mother saw that, her lamentations and outcries began in real earnest; she said she would far rather have had no child at all than have a donkey, and that they were to throw it into the water that the fishes might devour it. But the King said: "No, since God has sent him he shall be my son and heir, and after my death sit on the royal throne and wear the kingly crown."

The donkey, therefore, was brought up and grew bigger, and his ears grew up high and straight. And he was of a merry disposition, jumped about, played and took especial pleasure in music, so that he went to a celebrated musician and said: "Teach me your art, that I may play the lute as well as you do." "Ah, dear little master," answered the magician, "that would come very hard to you, your fingers are not quite suited to it, and are far too big. I am afraid the strings would not last." But no excuses were of any use – the donkey was determined to play the lute. And since he was persevering and industrious, he at last learnt to do it as well as the master himself.

The young lordling once went out walking full of thought and came to a well; he looked into it and in the mirror-clear water saw his donkey's form. He was so distressed about it that he went out into the wide world and only took with him one faithful companion. They travelled up and down, and at last they came into a kingdom where an old King reigned who had a single but wonderfully beautiful daughter. The donkey said: "Here we will stay," knocked at the gate, and cried: "A guest is without – open, that he may enter." When the gate was not opened, he sat down, took his lute and played it in the most delightful manner with his two fore-feet. Then the door-keeper opened his eyes, and gaped, and ran to the King and said:

"Outside by the gate sits a young donkey which plays the lute as well as an experienced master!" "Then let the musician come to me," said the King. But when a donkey came in, everyone began to laugh at the lute-player. And when the donkey was asked to sit down and eat with the servants, he was unwilling, and said: "I am no common stable-ass, I am a noble one." Then they said: "If that is what you are, seat yourself with the soldiers." "No, said he, I will sit by the King." The King smiled and said good-humouredly: "Yes, it shall be as you will, little ass, come here to me." Then he asked: "Little ass, how does my daughter please you?" The donkey turned his head towards her, looked at her, nodded and said: "I like her above measure, I have never yet seen anyone so beautiful as she is." "Well, then, you shall sit next her too", said the King. "That is exactly what I wish", said the donkey, and he placed himself by her side, ate and drank, and knew how to behave himself daintily and cleanly. When the noble beast had stayed a long time at the King's court, he thought: "What good does all this do me, I shall still have to go home again", let his head hang sadly, and went to the King and asked for his dismissal. But the King had grown fond of him, and said: "Little ass, what ails you? You look as sour as a jug of vinegar, I will give you what you want. Do you want gold?" "No", said the donkey, and shook his head. "Do you want jewels and rich dress?" "No". "Do you wish for half my kingdom?" "Indeed, no". Then said the King; "If I did but know what would make you content. Will you have my pretty daughter to wife?" "Ah, yes", said the ass, "I should indeed like her", and all at once he became quite merry and full of happiness, for that was exactly what he was wishing for. So a great and splendid wedding was held. In the evening, when the bride and bridegroom were led into their bed-room, the King wanted to know if the ass would behave well, and ordered a servant to hide himself there. When they were both within, the bridegroom bolted the door, looked around, and as he believed that they were quite alone, he suddenly threw off his ass's skin, and stood there in the form of a handsome royal youth. "Now", said he, "you see who I am, and see also that I am not unworthy of you". The bride was glad, and kissed him, and loved him dearly. When morning came, he jumped up, put his animal's skin on again, and no one could have guessed what kind of a form was hidden beneath it. Soon came the old King. "Ah", cried he, "so the little ass is already up! But surely you are sad" he said to his daughter, "that you have not got a proper man for your husband?" "Oh, no, dear father, I love him as well as if he were the handsomest in the world, and I will keep him as long as I live". The King was surprised, but the servant who had concealed himself came and revealed everything to him. The King said: "That cannot be true". "Then watch yourself the next night and you will see it with your own eyes; and hark you, lord King, if you were to take his skin away and throw it in the fire, he would be forced to show himself in his true shape". "Your advice is good", said the King, and at night when they were asleep, he stole in, and when he got to the bed he saw by the light of the moon a noble looking youth lying there, and the skin lay stretched on the ground. So he took it away and had a great fire lighted outside, and threw the skin into it, and remained by it himself until it was all burnt to ashes. But since he was anxious to know how the robbed man would behave himself, he stayed awake the whole night and watched. When the youth had slept his fill, he got up by the first light of morning and wanted to put on the ass's skin, but it was not to be found. At this he was alarmed, and, full of grief and anxiety, said: "Now I shall have to contrive to escape". But when he went out, there stood the King, who said: "My son, whither away in such haste? what have you in mind? Stay here, you are such a handsome man, you shall not go away from me. I will now give you half my kingdom, and after my death you shall have the whole of it. "Then I hope that what begins so well may end well, and I will stay with you", said the youth. And the old man gave him half the kingdom, and in a year's time, when he died, the youth had the whole, and after the death of his father he had another kingdom as well, and lived in all magnificence.

Jakob and Wilhelm Grimm
Grimm's Fairy Tales 1812–15

4. Donkeys Delinquent

ABOARD THE ARK

'Twas when the rain fell steady an' the Ark was pitched an' ready,
That Noah got his orders for to take the bastes below;
He dragged them all together by the horn an' hide an' feather,
An' all excipt the Donkey was agreeable to go.

First Noah spoke him fairly, thin talked to him sevairely,
An' thin he cursed him squarely to the glory av' the Lord
'Divil take the ass that bred you, and the greater ass that fed you!
'Divil go wid you, ye spalpeen!' an' the Donkey wint aboard.

But the wind was always failin', and 'twas most onaisy sailin',
An' the ladies in the cabin couldn't stand the stable air;
An' the bastes betwuxt the hatches, they tuk an' died in batches,
Till Noah said: – 'There's wan av us that hasn't paid his fare!'

For he heard a flusteration 'mid the bastes av all creation –
The trumpetin' av elephints an' bellowin' av whales;
An' he saw forninst the windy whin he wint to stop the shindy
The Divil wid a stable-fork bedivillin' their tails.

The Divil cursed outrageous, but Noah said umbrageous: –
'To what am I indebted for this tenant-right invasion?'
An' the Divil gave for answer: – 'Evict me if you can, sir,
For I came in wid the Donkey – on Your Honour's invitation.'

Rudyard Kipling
The Legends of Evil 1890

ODE TO MY ASS, PETER

Ah, Peter, I remember, oft, when tir'd
And most unpleasantly at times bemir'd,
Bold hast thou said, "I'll budge not one inch further:
And now, young master, you may kick or murther,
Then have I cugell'd thee – a fruitless matter!
For 'twas in vain to kick, or flog or chatter.
Though Balaam-like, I curs'd thee with a smack;
Sturdy thou dropp'd thine ears upon thy back,
And trotting retrograde, with wiggling tail,
In vain did I thy running rump assail:
For lo, between thy legs, thou putt'dst thine head,
And gavest me a puddle for my bed.
Now this was fair – the action bore no guile;
Thou duck'dst me not, like Judas, with a smile,
O were the manners of some monarchs *such*,
    Who smile ev'n in the close insiduous hour
    That kicks th'unguarded minion from his pow'r!
But this is asking p'rhaps of kings *too much*.

John Wolcot
The Works of Peter Pindar, Esq.
18th century

An 18th century print showing a donkey taking grain to the mill

STEALING THE SHOW

It was Dorcas, our Dorcas, that the crowd of hundreds looked at. She stole the show. The beautiful carriages, the gigs, the wagonette, the pair of Shetland ponies, the Eton donkey himself, went round and round unnoticed.

Our success was not one we had intended.

My husband and I, pleased with our brand-new turn-out, harness and paint shining in the sun, were pretty smart ourselves. He was wearing a good suit, with a bowler hat. To keep my soft silk hat on I had tied a headscarf over it under my chin, thus giving it, though this was unplanned, an appropriate Victorian-bonnet appearance.

It might not have happened if there had not been a slight rise in the ground a little beyond the entrance to the ring. Or if Dorcas had been more accustomed to her phaeton. A good deal of rain had fallen in the past few days, and motor vehicles in earlier events had made the going muddy and heavy. She had scarcely drawn this carriage at all, and then only on a hard surface. Besides, she was still cross.

Feeling the rise and the narrow wheels weighty in the mud, her trot slowed to a walk. This was no place – so her slowness, her unwillingness, clearly informed us – for any carriage. Other vehicles began to pass us. Then we had breasted the little rise: and the ground, if it was not dead level, was now going down. This no longer mattered to Dorcas. Suddenly, for the first time in our knowledge of her, she became pure, obstinate Donkey.

Not one inch would she move. I cajoled, flapped reins, urged – and the crowd howled with joy. My husband jumped down and, going to her head, tried to pull her forward. This proving as unavailing as trying to shift a growing tree, he took off his bowler hat, and behind it pretended to whisper in Dorcas's long ear. At this the audience, ranked ten and twelve deep round the ringside, already swaying with noisy mirth and cheering us on, became practically hysterical. I myself was laughing so much that the muscles of my arms were useless and I could hardly hold the reins, let alone continue with my urging.

Only at a circus, when the clowns have been in the ring, have I heard such prolonged, huge laughter from a great crowd. Clowns we were indeed. My husband played up to the part thrust upon him; and of course the bowler hat, a headgear so little associated with donkeys, added the final perfect touch of comedy.

From the corner of my eye I saw the other carriages going round and round, drawing out to pass us; the same ones coming round again, and again; drawing out wider now as the local news television cameras closed in on us. . . .

A pair of donkeys in harness shown by Miss Burdett-Coutts at the Agricultural Hall, Islington in 1865

The shouting, the laughter roaring like tumultuous seas, the whirring of cameras: to these as to the pulling, the persuading, the ear-whispering, Dorcas remained immovably, stolidly, indifferent. She might have been standing motionless in an empty field. . . .

The ring was needed for the next event. The other carriages filed out, a few of the drivers perhaps understandably piqued that attention had been so absurdly, so clownishly, diverted from them.

Still Dorcas could not be enticed to budge.

It took two strong men to force her at last to yield. Assisted by her master pulling at her head, they pushed the phaeton from behind. All the way to the ring entrance – quite a distance – they had to push, Dorcas stumbling reluctantly forward. Not until she was out of the enclosure did she agree to pull, and biddably went back to the unharnessing line.

Doris Rybot
My Kingdom for a Donkey 1963

BILL'S DONKEY

If I had a donkey wot wouldn't go
D'ye think I'd wallop him? – no, no, no;
But gentle means I'd try, d'ye see,
Because I hate all cruelty:
If all had been like me, in fact,
There'd ha' been no occasion for Martin's Act,[1]
Dumb animals to prevent getting crack'd
                    On the head.
For if I had a donkey wot wouldn't go,
I never would wallop him, no, no, no;
I'd give him some hay, and cry, Gee O!
                    And Come up, Neddy!

What makes me mention this, this morn
I see'd that cruel chap, Bill Burn,
Whilst he was out a'crying his greens,
His donkey wallop with all his means:
He hit him over the head and thighs,
And brought the tears up on his eyes;
At last my blood began to rise,
                    And I said –
    If I had a donkey etc.

Bill turn'd and said to me, "Then perhaps
You're one of these Mr Martin chaps,
Wot now is seeking for occasion
All for to lie a hinformation."
Though this I stoutly did deny,
Bill up and gave me a blow in the eye,
And I replied, as I let fly
At his head –
If I had a donkey etc.

As Bill and I did break the peace,
To us came up the New Police,[2]
And hiked us off, as sure as fate,
Afore the sitting magistrate:
I told his worship all the spree,
And for to prove my veracity,
I wish'd he would the animal see,
For I said –
If I had a donkey, etc.

Bill's donkey was ordered into court,
In which he caused a deal of sport;
He cock'd his ears and op'd his jaws;
As if he wished to plead his cause.
I proved I'd been uncommonly kind,
The ass got a verdict – Bill got fined;
For his worship and I were of one mind:
And he said –
If I had a donkey, etc.

Anonymous
19th century

1. *Richard Martin was instrumental in bringing into law in 1822 an Act "to prevent the cruel and improper treatment of cattle". He was a founder member of the R.S.P.C.A.*

2. *Sir Robert Peel created the Metropolitan Police Force in 1829.*

"DONKEYS, JANET"

Janet had gone away to get the bath ready, when my aunt, to my great alarm, became in one moment rigid with indignation, and had hardly voice to cry out, "Janet! Donkeys!"

Upon which, Janet came running up the stairs as if the house were in flames, darted out on a little piece of green in front, and warned off two saddle-donkeys, lady-ridden, that had presumed to set hoof upon it; while my aunt, rushing out of the house, seized the bridle of a third animal laden with a bestriding child, turned him, led him forth from those sacred precincts, and boxed the ears of the unlucky urchin in attendance who had dared to profane that hallowed ground.

To this hour I don't know whether my aunt had any lawful right of way over that patch of green: but she had settled it in her own mind that she had, and it was all the same to her. The one great outrage of her life, demanding to be constantly avenged, was the passage of a donkey over that immaculate spot. In whatever occupation she was engaged, however interesting to her the conversation in which she was taking part, a donkey turned the current of her ideas in a moment, and she was upon him straight. Jugs of water, and watering pots, were kept in secret places ready to be discharged on the offending boys: sticks were laid in ambush behind the door; sallies were made at all hours; and incessant war prevailed. Perhaps this was an agreeable excitement to the donkey-boys: or perhaps the more sagacious of the donkeys, understanding how the case stood, delighted with constitutional obstinacy in coming that way. I only know that there were three alarms before the bath was ready; and that on the occasion of the last and most desperate of all, I saw my aunt engage, single-handed, with a sandy-headed lad of fifteen, and bump his sandy head against her own gate, before he seemed to comprehend what was the matter. These interruptions were the more ridiculous to me, because she was giving me broth out of a table-spoon at the time (having firmly persuaded herself that I was actually starving, and must receive nourishment at first in very small quantities), and while my mouth was yet open to receive the spoon she would put it back in the basin, cry "Janet! Donkeys!" and go out to the assault.

My aunt was a little more imperious and stern than usual, but I observed no other token of her preparing herself to receive the visitor so much dreaded by me. She sat at work in the window, and I sat by, with my thoughts running astray on all possible and impossible results of Mr. Murdstone's visit, until pretty late in the afternoon. Our dinner had been indefinitely postponed; but it was growing so late that my aunt had ordered it to be got ready, when she gave a sudden alarm of donkeys, and to my consternation and amazement I beheld Miss Murdstone, on a side-saddle, ride deliberately over the sacred piece of green and stop in front of the house, looking about her.

"Go along with you!" cried my aunt, shaking her head and her fist at the window. "You have no business there. How dare you trespass? Go along! Oh! you bold-faced thing!"

My aunt was so exasperated by the coolness with which Miss Murdstone looked about her, that I really believe she was motionless and unable for the moment to dart out according to custom. I seized the opportunity to inform her who it was; and that the gentleman now coming near the offender (for the way up was very steep and he had dropped behind) was Mr. Murdstone himself.

"I don't care who it is!" cried my aunt, still shaking her head, and gesticulating anything but welcome from the bow-window. "I won't be trespassed upon. I won't allow it. Go away! Janet, turn him round. Lead him off!" and I saw, from behind my aunt, a sort of hurried battle-piece, in which the donkey stood resisting everybody, with all his four legs planted different ways, while Janet tried to pull him round by the bridle, Mr. Murdstone tried to lead him on, Miss Murdstone struck at Janet with a parasol, and several boys, who had come to see the engagement, shouted vigorously. But my aunt, suddenly descrying among them the young malefactor who was the donkey's guardian, and who was one of the most inveterate offenders against her, though hardly in his teens, rushed out to the scene of action, pounced upon him, captured him, dragged him, with his jacket over his head and his heels grinding the ground, into the garden, and calling upon Janet to fetch the constables and justices, that he might be taken, tried and executed on the spot, held him at bay there. This part of the business, however, did not last long; for the young rascal, being expert at a variety of feints and dodges, of which my aunt had no conception, soon went whooping away, leaving some deep depressions of his nailed boots in the flower-beds and taking his donkey in triumph with him.

Charles Dickens
David Copperfield 1849

THE ASS IN MAY

The ass beneath his bags of sand
Oft jerks the string from leader's hand
And on the road will eager stoop
To pick the sprouting thistle up
Oft answering on his weary way
Some distant neighbour's sobbing bray
Dinning the ears of driving boy
As if he felt a fit of joy
Within its pinfold circle left
Of all its company bereft.

John Clare
The Shepheard's Calendar 1827

AT THE JULY FEAST

And long-eared racers, fam'd for sport and fun,
Appear this day to have their swiftness tried;
Where some won't start, and Dick, the race nigh won,
Enamour'd of some Jenny by his side,
Forgets the winning post to court a bride;
In vain the rout urge on the jockey-clown
To lump his cudgel on his harden'd hide,
Ass after ass still hee-haws through the town,
And in disgrace at last each jockey bumps adown.

John Clare *1819*

If I had a donkey
That wouldn't go,
D'you think I'd wallop him?
No! No! No!

I'd put him in a stable
And keep him nice and warm,
The best little donkey
That ever was born.

Gee up, Neddy,
Gee up, Neddy,
The best little donkey
That ever was born.

Nursery Rhyme

DALLIANCE WITH DONKEYS

"What do you think of doing with yourself this morning?" inquired the captain. "Shall we lunch at Pegwell?"

"I should like that very much indeed", interposed Mrs. Tuggs. She had never heard of Pegwell; but the word "lunch" had reached her ears, and it sounded very agreeably.

"How shall we go?" inquired the captain; "it's too warm to walk."

"A shay?" suggested Mr. Joseph Tuggs.

"Chaise", whispered Mr. Cymon.

"I should think one would be enough", said Mr. Joseph Tuggs aloud, quite unconscious of the meaning of the correction. "However, two shays if you like."

"I should like a donkey *so* much", said Belinda.

"Oh, so should I!" echoed Charlotta Tuggs.

"Well, we can have a fly", suggested the captain, "and you can have a couple of donkeys."

A fresh difficulty arose. Mrs. Captain Waters declared it would be decidedly improper for two ladies to ride alone. The remedy was obvious. Perhaps young Mr. Tuggs would be gallant enough to accompany them.

Mr. Cymon Tuggs blushed, smiled, looked vacant, and faintly protested that he was no horseman. The objection was at once overruled. A fly was speedily found; and three donkeys – which the proprietor declared on his solemn asseveration to be "three parts blood, and the other corn" – were engaged in the service.

"Kim up!" shouted one of the two boys who followed behind, to propel the donkeys, when Belinda Waters and Charlotta Tuggs had been hoisted, and pushed, and pulled, into their respective saddles.

"Hi-hi-hi!" groaned the other boy behind Mr. Cymon Tuggs. Away went the donkey, with the stirrups jingling against the heels of Cymon's boots, and Cymon's boots nearly scraping the ground.

"Way-way! Wo-o-o-o-!" cried Mr. Cymon Tuggs as well as he could, in the midst of the jolting.

"Don't make it gallop!" screamed Mrs. Captain Waters, behind.

"My donkey *will* go into the public-house!" shrieked Miss Tuggs in the rear.

"Hi-hi-hi!" groaned both the boys together; and on went the donkeys as if nothing would ever stop them.

Everything has an end, however; even the galloping of donkeys will cease in time. The animal which Mr. Cymon Tuggs bestrode, feeling sundry uncomfortable tugs at the bit, the intent of which he could by no means divine, abruptly sidled against a brick wall, and expressed his uneasiness by grinding Mr. Cymon Tugg's leg on the rough surface. Mrs. Captain Waters's donkey, apparently under the influence of some playfulness of spirit, rushed suddenly, head first, into a hedge and declined to come out again: and the quadruped on which Miss Tuggs was mounted expressed his delight at this humorous proceeding by firmly planting his fore-feet against the ground, and kicking up his hind legs in a very agile, but somewhat alarming manner.

This abrupt termination to the rapidity of the ride naturally occasioned some confusion. Both the ladies indulged in vehement screaming for several minutes; and Mr. Cymon Tuggs, besides sustaining intense bodily pain, had the additional mental anguish of witnessing their distressing situation, without having the power to rescue them, by reason of his leg being firmly screwed in between the animal and the wall. The efforts of the boys, however, assisted by the ingenious expedient of twisting the tail of the most rebellious donkey, restored order in a much shorter time than could have reasonably been expected, and the little party jogged on slowly together.

"Now let 'em walk", said Mr. Cymon Tuggs. "It's cruel to overdrive 'em."

"Werry well, sir", replied the boy, with a grin at his companion, as if he understood Mr. Cymon to mean that the cruelty applied less to the animals than to their riders.

"What a lovely day, dear!" said Charlotta.

"Charming, enchanting, dear!" responded Mrs. Captain Waters. "What a beautiful prospect, Mr. Tuggs!"

Cymon looked full into Belinda's face, as he responded – "Beautiful, indeed!" The lady cast down her eyes, and suffered the animal she was riding to fall a little back. Cymon Tuggs instinctively did the same.

There was a brief silence, broken only by a sigh from Mr. Cymon Tuggs.

"Mr. Cymon", said the lady suddenly, in a low tone, "Mr. Cymon – I am another's."

Mr. Cymon expressed his perfect concurrence in a statement which it was impossible to controvert.

"If I had not been . . ." resumed Belinda; and there she stopped.

"What – what?" said Mr. Cymon earnestly. "Do not torture me. What would you say?"

"If I had not been" – continued Mrs. Captain Waters – "if, in earlier life it had been my fate to have known, and been beloved by, a noble youth – a kindred soul – a congenial spirit – one capable of feeling and appreciating the sentiments which . . ."

"Heavens! what do I hear?" exclaimed Mr. Cymon Tuggs. "Is it possible! can I believe my – Come up!" (This last unsentimental parenthesis was

'Morning Promenade upon the Cliff, Brighton',
coloured etching after J. Morse, 1806

addressed to the donkey, who, with his head between his fore-legs, appeared to be examining the state of his shoes with great anxiety.

"Hi-hi-hi", said the boys behind. "Come up", expostulated Cymon Tuggs again. "Hi-hi-hi", repeated the boys. And whether it was that the animal felt indignant at the tone of Mr. Tuggs's command, or felt alarmed by the noise of the deputy proprietor's boots running behind him; or whether he burned with a noble emulation to outstrip the other donkeys; certain it is that he no sooner heard the second series of "hi-hi's", than he started away, with a celerity of pace which jerked Mr. Cymon's hat off, instantaneously, and carried him to the Pegwell Bay hotel in no time, where he deposited his rider without giving him the trouble of dismounting, by sagaciously pitching him over his head, into the very doorway of the tavern.

Great was the confusion of Mr. Cymon Tuggs, when he was put, right end uppermost, by two waiters; considerable was the alarm of Mrs. Tuggs in behalf of her son; agonizing were the apprehensions of Mrs. Captain Waters on his account. It was speedily discovered, however, that he had not sustained much more injury than the donkey – he was grazed, and the animal was grazing – and then it *was* a delightful party to be sure! Mr. and Mrs. Tuggs, and the captain, had ordered lunch in the little garden behind: small saucers of large shrimps, dabs of butter, crusty loaves, and bottled ale. The sky was without a cloud; there were flower-pots and turf before them; the sea, from the foot of the cliff, stretching away as far as the eye could discern anything at all; vessels in this distance with sails as white, and as small, as nicely-got-up handkerchiefs. The shrimps were delightful, the ale better, and the captain even more pleasant than either. Mrs. Captain Waters was in *such* spirits after lunch! – chasing, first the captain across the turf and among the flower-pots; and then Mr. Cymon Tuggs; and then Miss Tuggs; and laughing, too, quite boisterously. But as the captain said, it didn't matter; who knew what they were, there? For all the people of the house knew, they might be common people. To which Mr. Joseph Tuggs responded, "To be sure." And then they went down the steep wooden steps a little further on, which led to the bottom of the cliff; and looked at the crabs, and the seaweed, and the eels, till it was more than fully time to go back to Ramsgate again. Finally, Mr. Cymon Tuggs ascended the steps last, and Mrs. Captain Waters last but one; and Mr. Cymon Tuggs discovered that the foot and ankle of Mrs. Captain Waters were even more unexceptionable than he had at first supposed.

Taking a donkey towards his ordinary place of residence is a very different thing, and a feat much more easily to be accomplished, than taking him from it. It requires a great deal of foresight and presence of mind in the one case, to anticipate the numerous flights of his discursive imagination; whereas, in the other, all you have to do, is to hold on and place a blind confidence in the animal. Mr. Cymon Tuggs adopted the latter expedient on his return; and his nerves were so little discomposed by the journey that he distinctly understood they were all to meet again at the library in the evening.

Charles Dickens
Sketches by Boz 1867

"DALESMAN" AND HIS FIRST HUNTER

Why, you may inquire, my interest in donkeys? Well, let me tell you, for now on these winter evenings, with the winds from the west starting out on their long journeys from this very place, and the peat smoke whirling up the chimney, I sit and remember, as old men do, the far, far away days of childhood.

When I was very little, my father paid a man two pounds for a donkey at a fair. It became my most treasured possession, apart from being extremely useful about the place. There being no motor mowers or small trucks to ease the burdens around the home, he performed the donkey work.

However, he was not what might be called a "good hunter", and although I used to ride him with the harriers he sometimes earned a black mark. On his first outing, walking among the hounds at the meet and braying loudly, he so scattered them that they were collected only with difficulty – and that only after someone had caught the whipper-in's horse.

Then, of course, not being very fast he was never in the first flight. Thus when the hare made a circle, as hares so often will, he was going around the first lap when he was overtaken, or else he headed the hare, as the case might be.

Many horses did not appreciate him, either, and after an encounter with a rather pompous soldier of the older school at the corner of a covert, resulting with his horse bolting with him through some impenetrable thickets, the suggestion to my father that I had a pony was agreed upon, to save further worry.

C. N. de Courcy Parry ("Dalesman") *1974*

MODESTINE

There dwelt an old man in Monastier, of rather unsound intellect according to some, much followed by street-boys, and known to fame as Father Adam. Father Adam had a cart, and to draw the cart a diminutive she-ass, not much bigger than a dog, the colour of a mouse, with a kindly eye and a determined under-jaw. There was something neat and high-bred, a quakerish elegance, about the rogue that hit my fancy on the spot. Our first interview was in Monastier market-place. To prove her good temper, one child after another was set upon her back to ride, and one after another went head over heels into the air; until a want of confidence began to reign in youthful bosoms, and the experiment was discontinued from a dearth of subjects. I was already backed by a deputation of my friends; but as if this were not enough, all the buyers and sellers came round and helped me in the bargain; and the ass and I and Father Adam were the centre of a hubbub for near half an hour. At length she passed into my service for the consideration of sixty-five francs and a glass of brandy. The sack had already cost eighty francs and two glasses of beer; so that Modestine, as I instantly baptised her, was upon all counts the cheaper article. Indeed, that was as it should be; for she was only an appurtenance of my mattress, or self-acting bedstead on four castors.

I had a last interview with Father Adam in a billiard-room at the witching hour of dawn, when I administered the brandy. He professed himself greatly touched by the separation, and declared he had often bought white bread for the donkey when he had been content with black bread for himself; but this, according to the best authorities, must have been a flight of fancy. He had a name in the village for brutally misusing the ass; yet it is certain that he shed a tear, and the tear made a clean mark down one cheek. . . .

On the day of my departure I was up a little after five; by six, we began to load the donkey; and ten minutes after, my hopes were in the dust. The pad would not stay on Modestine's back for half a moment. I returned it to its maker, with whom I had so contumelious a passage that the street outside was crowded from wall to wall with gossips looking on and listening. The pad changed hands with much vivacity; perhaps it would be more descriptive to say that we threw it at each other's heads; and at any rate, we were very warm and unfriendly, and spoke with a deal of freedom.

I had a common donkey pack-saddle – a *barde*, as they call it – fitted upon Modestine; and once more loaded her with my effects. The doubled sack, my pilot-coat (for it was warm, and I was to walk in my waistcoat), a great bar of black bread and an open basket containing the white bread, the mutton and the bottles, were all corded together in a very elaborate system of knots, and I looked on the result with fatuous content. In such a monstrous deck-cargo, all poised above the donkey's shoulders, with nothing below to balance, on a brand-new pack-saddle that had not yet been worn to fit the animal, and fastened with brand-new girths that might be expected to stretch and slacken by the way, even a very careless traveller should have seen disaster brewing. That elaborate system of knots, again, was the work of too many sympathisers to be very artfully designed. It is true they tightened the cords with a will; as many as three at a time would have a foot against Modestine's quarters and be hauling with clenched teeth; but I learned afterwards that one thoughtful person, without any exercise of force, can make a more solid job than half a dozen heated and enthusiastic grooms. I was then but a novice; even after the misadventure of the pad nothing could disturb my security, and I went forth from the stable-door as an ox goeth to the slaughter.

The bell of Monastier was just striking nine as I got quit of these preliminary troubles and descended the hill through the common. As long as I was within sight of the windows, a secret shame and the fear of some laughable defeat withheld me from tampering with Modestine. She tripped along upon her four small hoofs with a sober daintiness of gait; from time to time she shook her ears or her tail; and she looked so small under the bundle that my mind misgave me. We got across the ford without difficulty – there was no doubt about the matter, she was docility itself – and once on the other bank, where the road begins to mount through pine-woods, I took in my right hand the unhallowed staff, and with a quaking spirit applied it to the donkey. Modestine brisked up her pace for perhaps three steps, and then relapsed into her former minuet. Another application had the same effect, and so with the third. I am worthy the name of an Englishman, and it goes against my conscience to lay my hand rudely on a female. I desisted, and looked her all over from head to foot; the poor brute's knees were trembling and her breathing was distressed; it was plain that she could go no faster on a hill. God forbid, thought I, that I should brutalise this innocent creature; let her go at her own pace, and let me patiently follow.

What that pace was, there is no word mean enough to describe; it was something as much slower than a walk as a walk is slower than a run; it kept me hanging on each foot for an incredible length of time; in five minutes it exhausted the spirit and set up a fever in all the muscles of the leg. And yet I had to keep close at hand and measure my advance exactly upon hers; for if I dropped a few yards into the rear, or went on a few yards ahead, Modestine came instantly to a halt and began to browse. The thought that this was to last from here to Alais nearly broke my heart. Of all conceivable journeys, this promised to be the most tedious. I tried to tell myself it was a lovely day;

I tried to charm my foreboding spirit with tobacco; but I had a vision ever present to me of the long, long roads, up hill and down dale, and a pair of figures ever infinitesimally moving, foot by foot, a yard to the minute, and, like things enchanted in a nightmare, approaching no nearer to the goal.

In the meantime there came up behind us a tall peasant, perhaps forty years of age, of an ironical snuffy countenance, and arrayed in the greentail-coat of the country. He overtook us hand over hand, and stopped to consider our pitiful advance.

"Your donkey", says he, "is very old?"

I told him I believed not.

Then, he supposed, we had come far.

I told him we had but newly left Monastier.

"*Et vous marchez comme ça*!" cried he; and throwing back his head, he laughed long and heartily. I watched him, half prepared to feel offended, until he had satisfied his mirth; and then, "You must have no pity on these animals", said he; and, plucking a switch out of a thicket, he began to lace Modestine about the stern-works, uttering a cry. The rogue pricked up her ears and broke into a good round pace, which she kept up without flagging, and without exhibiting the least symptom of distress, as long as the peasant

kept beside us. Her former panting and shaking had been, I regret to say, a piece of comedy.

My *deus ex machina,* before he left me, supplied some excellent, if inhumane, advice; presented me with the switch, which he declared she would feel more tenderly than my cane; and finally taught me the true cry or masonic word of donkey-drivers, "Proot!" All the time, he regarded me with a comical incredulous air which was embarrassing to confront; and smiled over my donkey-driving as I might have smiled over his orthography, or his green tailcoat. But it was not my turn for the moment.

I was proud of my new lore and thought I had learned the art to perfection. And certainly Modestine did wonders for the rest of the forenoon and I had a breathing space to look about me. . . .

In this pleasant humour I came down the hill to where Goudet stands in the green end of a valley, with Château Beaufort opposite upon a rocky steep, and the stream, as clear as crystal, lying in a deep pool between them. Above and below, you may hear it wimpling over the stones, an amiable stripling of a river, which it seems absurd to call the Loire. . . .

I hurried over my midday meal and was early forth again. But, alas, as we climbed the interminable hill upon the other side, "Proot!" seemed to

have lost its virtue. I prooted like a lion, I prooted mellifluously like a sucking dove; but Modestine would be neither softened nor intimidated. She held doggedly to her pace; nothing but a blow would move her, and that only for a second. I must follow at her heels, incessantly belabouring. A moment's pause in this ignoble toil, and she relapsed into her own private gait. I think I never heard of anyone in as mean a situation. I must reach the lake of Bouchet, where I meant to camp, before sundown, and, to have even a hope of this, I must instantly maltreat this uncomplaining animal. The sound of my own blows sickened me. Once, when I looked at her, she had a faint resemblance to a lady of my acquaintance who formerly loaded me with kindness; and this increased my horror of my cruelty.

To make matters worse, we encountered another donkey, ranging at will upon the roadside; and this other donkey chanced to be a gentleman. He and Modestine met nickering for joy, and I had to separate the pair and beat down their young romance with a renewed and feverish bastinado. If the other donkey had had the heart of a male under his hide, he would have fallen upon me tooth and hoof; and this was a kind of consolation – he was plainly unworthy of Modestine's affection. But the incident saddened me, as did everything that spoke of my donkey's sex.

It was blazing hot up the valley, windless, with vehement sun upon my shoulders; and I had to labour so consistently with my stick that the sweat ran into my eyes. Every five minutes, too, the pack, the basket and the pilot-coat would take an ugly slew to one side or the other; and I had to stop Modestine just when I had got her to a tolerable pace of about two miles an hour, to tug, push, shoulder and readjust the load. And at last, in the village of Ussel, saddle and all, the whole hypothec turned round and grovelled in the dust below the donkeys's belly. She, none better pleased, incontinently drew up and seemed to smile; and a party of one man, two women and two children came up, and, standing round me in a half-circle, encouraged her by their example.

I had the devil's own trouble to get the thing righted; and the instant I had done so, without hesitation, it toppled and fell down upon the other side. Judge if I was hot! And yet not a hand was offered to assist me. The man, indeed, told me I ought to have a package of a different shape. I suggested, if he knew nothing better to the point in my predicament, he might hold his tongue. And the good-natured dog agreed with me smilingly. It was the most despicable fix. I must plainly content myself with the pack for Modestine, and take the following items for my own share of the portage: a cane, a quart flask, a pilot-jacket heavily weighted in the pockets, two pounds of black bread and an open basket full of meats and bottles. I believe I may say I am not devoid of greatness of soul; for I did not recoil from this infamous burden.

I disposed it, Heaven knows how, so as to be mildly portable, and then proceeded to steer Modestine through the village. She tried, as was indeed her invariable habit, to enter every house and every courtyard in the whole length; and, encumbered as I was, without a hand to help myself, no words can render an idea of my difficulties. A priest, with six or seven others, was examining a church in process of repair, and he and his acolytes laughed loudly as they saw my plight. I remembered having laughed myself when I had seen good men struggling with adversity in the person of a jackass, and the recollection filled me with penitence. That was in my old light days, before this trouble came upon me. God knows at least that I shall never laugh again, thought I. But oh, what a cruel thing is a farce to those engaged in it!

A little out of the village, Modestine, filled with the demon, set her heart upon a by-road, and positively refused to leave it. I dropped all my bundles, and, I am ashamed to say, struck the poor sinner twice across the face. It was pitiful to see her lift up her head with shut eyes, as if waiting for another blow. I came very near crying; but I did a wiser thing than that, and sat squarely down by the roadside to consider my situation under the cheerful influence of tobacco and a nip of brandy. Modestine, in the meanwhile, munched some black bread with a contrite, hypocritical air. It was plain that I must make a sacrifice to the gods of shipwreck. I threw away the empty bottle destined to carry milk; I threw away my own white bread and, disdaining to act by general average, kept the black bread for Modestine; lastly, I threw away the cold leg of mutton and the egg-whisk, although this last was dear to my heart. Thus I found room for everything in the basket and even stowed the boating-coat on the top. By means of an end of cord I slung it under one arm; and although the cord cut my shoulder and the jacket hung almost to the ground, it was with a heart greatly lightened that I set forth again.

I had now an arm free to thrash Modestine and cruelly I chastised her. If I were to reach the lakeside before dark she must bestir her little shanks to some tune. Already the sun had gone down into a windy-looking mist; and although there were still a few streaks of gold far off to the east on the hills and the black fir-woods, all was cold and grey about our onward path. An infinity of little country by-roads led hither and thither among the fields. It was the most pointless labyrinth. I could see my destination overhead, or rather the peak that dominates it, but choose as I pleased, the road always ended by turning away from it and sneaking back towards the valley or northward along the margin of the hills. The failing light, the waning colour, the naked, unhomely, stony country through which I was travelling, threw me into some despondency. I promise you, the stick was not idle; I think every decent step that Modestine took must have cost me at least two emphatic blows. There was not another sound in the neighbourhood but that of my unwearying bastinado.

Suddenly, in the midst of my toils, the load once more bit the dust, and, as by enchantment, all the cords were simultaneously loosened and the road scattered with my dear possessions. The packing was to begin again from the beginning; and as I had to invent a new and better system, I do not doubt but I lost half an hour. It began to be dusk in earnest as I reached a wilderness of turf and stones. It had the air of being a road which should lead everywhere at the same time; and I was falling into something not unlike despair when I saw two figures stalking towards me over the stones. They walked one behind the other like tramps, but their pace was remarkable. The son led the way, a tall, ill-made, sombre Scottish-looking man; the mother followed, all in her Sunday's best, with an elegantly embroidered ribbon to her cap, and a new felt hat atop, and proffering, as she strode along with kilted petticoats, a string of obscene and blasphemous oaths.

I hailed the son and asked him my direction. He pointed loosely west and north-west, muttered an inaudible comment, and, without slackening his pace for an instant, stalked on, as he was going, right athwart my path. The mother followed without as much as raising her head. I shouted and shouted after them, but they continued to scale the hillside and turned a deaf ear to my outcries. At least, leaving Modestine by herself, I was constrained to run after them, hailing the while. They stopped as I drew near, the mother cursing; and I could see she was a handsome, motherly, respectable-looking woman. The son once more answered me roughly and inaudibly, and was for setting out again. But this time I simply collared the mother, who was nearest me, and, apologising for my violence, declared that I could not let them go until they had put me on my road. They were neither of them offended – rather mollified than otherwise; told me I had only to follow them; and then the mother asked me what I wanted by the lake at such an hour. I replied, in the Scottish manner, by enquiring if she had far to go herself. She told me, with another oath, that she had an hour and a half's road before her. And then, without salutation, the pair strode forward again up the hillside in the gathering dusk.

I returned for Modestine, pushed her briskly forward and, after a sharp ascent of twenty minutes, reached the edge of a plateau. The view, looking back on my day's journey, was both wild and sad. Mount Mézenc and the peaks beyond St. Julien stood out in trenchant gloom against a cold glitter in the east; and the intervening field of hills had fallen together into one broad wash of shadow, except here and there the outline of a wooded sugar-loaf in black, here and there a white irregular patch to represent a cultivated farm, and here and there a blot where the Loire, the Gazeille or the Lausonne wandered in a gorge.

Soon we were on a highroad, and surprise seized on my mind as I beheld a village of some magnitude close at hand; for I had been told that the neighbourhood of the lake was uninhabited except by trout. The road smoked in the twilight with children driving home cattle from the fields; and a pair of mounted stride-legged women, hat and cap and all, dashed past me at a hammering trot from the canton where they had been to church and market. I asked one of the children where I was. At Bouchet St. Nicolas, he told me. Thither, about a mile south of my destination, and on the other side of a respectable summit, had these confused roads and treacherous peasantry conducted me. My shoulder was cut, so that it hurt sharply; my arm ached like toothache from perpetual beating; I gave up the lake and my design to camp, and asked for the *auberge*.

The *auberge* of Bouchet St. Nicolas was amongst the least pretentious I have ever visited; but I saw many more of the like upon my journey. Indeed, it was typical of these French highlands . . . but the people of the inn, in nine cases out of ten, show themselves friendly and considerate . . . I was tightly cross-examined about my journey . . .

"In the morning", said the husband, "I will make you something better than your cane. Such a beast as that feels nothing; it is in the proverb – *dur comme un âne*; you might beat her insensible with a cudgel, and yet you would arrive nowhere."

Something better! I little knew what he was offering . . .

I was up first in the morning (Monday, September 23rd). . . . It was five in the morning, and four thousand feet above the sea; and I had to bury my hands in my pockets and trot. People were coming out to the labours of the field by twos and threes, and all turned round to stare upon the stranger. I had seen them coming back last night, I saw them going afield again: and there was the life of Bouchet in a nutshell.

When I came back to the inn for a bit of breakfast the landlady was in the kitchen . . . "And where", said I, "is monsieur?"

"The master of the house is upstairs", she answered, "making you a goad."

Blessed be the man who invented goads! Blessed the innkeeper of Bouchet St. Nicolas, who introduced me to their use! This plain wand, with an eighth of an inch of pin, was indeed a sceptre when he put it in my hands. Thenceforward Modestine was my slave. A prick, and she passed the most inviting stable-door. A prick, and she broke forth into a gallant little trotlet that devoured the miles. It was not a remarkable speed, when all was said; and we took four hours to cover ten miles at the best of it. But what a heavenly change since yesterday! No more wielding of the ugly cudgel; no more flailing with an aching arm; no more broadsword exercise, but a discreet and gentlemanly fence. And what although now and then a drop of blood should appear on Modestine's mouse-coloured wedge-like rump? I should have preferred it otherwise, indeed; but yesterday's exploits had purged my heart of all humanity. The perverse little devil, since she would not be taken with kindness, must even go with pricking. . . .

On examination, on the morning of October 4th, Modestine was pronounced unfit for travel. She would need at least two days' repose according to the ostler; but I was now eager to reach Alais for my letters; and, being in a civilised country of stage-coaches, I determined to sell my lady friend and be off by the diligence that afternoon. Our yesterday's march, with the testimony of the driver who had pursued us up the long hill of St. Pierre, spread a favourable notion of my donkey's capabilities. Intending purchasers were aware of an unrivalled opportunity. Before ten I had an offer of twenty-five francs; and before noon, after a desperate engagement, I sold her, saddle and all, for five-and thirty. The pecuniary gain is not obvious, but I had bought freedom into the bargain. . . .

It was not until I was fairly seated by the driver, and rattling through a rocky valley with dwarf olives, that I became aware of my bereavement. I had lost Modestine. Up to that moment I had thought I hated her; but now she was gone.

"And, Oh,
The difference to me!"

For twelve days we had been fast companions; we had travelled upwards of a hundred and twenty miles, crossed several respectable ridges, and jogged along with our six legs by many a rocky and many a boggy by-road. After the first day, although sometimes I was hurt and distant in manner, I still kept my patience; and as for her, poor soul, she had come to regard me as a god. She loved to eat out of my hand. She was patient, elegant in form, the colour of an ideal mouse, and inimitably small. Her faults were those of her race and sex; her virtues were her own. Farewell, and if forever. . . .

Father Adam wept when he sold her to me; after I had sold her in my turn, I was tempted to follow his example; and being alone with a stage-driver and four or five agreeable young men, I did not hesitate to yield to my emotion.

Robert Louis Stevenson
Travels with a Donkey in the Cevennes 1896

5. Donkey Deals

AT THE FAIR

"I know where I'd get
An ass that would do,
If I had the money –
A pound or two,"

Said a ragged man
To my uncle one day;
He got the money
And went on his way.

And after that time
In market or fair
I'd look at the asses
That might be there

And wonder what kind
Of an ass would do
For a ragged man
With a pound or two.

Padraic Colum

'Village Horse Fair' by Edward Robert Smythe, 1810–1899

MY LITTLE BLACK ASS

It was in Kinvara that I first made acquaintance with my little black ass. It was a fair day, and he was standing beside a fence with his back to the weather – heedless of the world, and the world heedless of him. From the first moment that I laid my eye on him I admired him. I wanted an ass, for I was weary of tramping, and wouldn't this little fellow carry myself, my bag, my great coat and my other knick-knacks? And, thought I, I may get him cheap.

I inquired for his owner, but I searched the town before I found him, in front of a public-house, singing ballads for pennies. What! Sell the ass? Why shouldn't he sell him if he got his value? Yes, his value, and not a penny piece more than his value did he want; and only that the times were so bad he would never part with him – no fear! A fine young ass that could easily cover twenty miles a day. If he got a handful of oats once a month there wouldn't be a racehorse in the land that would hold a candle to him – not a horse!

Together we examined the "points" of the animal. What praise the owner gave him! There never was another ass, since the first ass came to Ireland, he assured me, so hearty, so sensible, and so far-seeing as he is.

"Do you know a habit he has?" said this master of the arts of praise; "if you gave him a little grain of oats in the morning, he would put some of it to keep fearing a scarcity next day – by all the holy books in Rome, he would." Somebody laughed. The tramp faced him; "What are you laughing at, you simpleton?" said the tinker. "He is so wise that he stores away a part of his food; isn't it often I was in such straits myself that I had to steal from him. Only for that ass it is often my twelve children and myself would be hungry!"

I inquired casually if this wise ass of his could distinguish between his master's and his neighbour's oats.

"He's as honest as the priest", said the man; "if all animals were like him, there would be no need for fence or trench, hedge or moat – not the smallest need."

A huge crowd had gathered round us by this time. The tinker's own children were there – I am not sure if the dozen were present, but the kind of youngsters that were there you wouldn't meet anywhere else in Ireland. A ragged, dirty, greasy set of children; and each surpassing the others in ill-manners. His wife was there, barefooted, hatless, wild.

"Peter", she said, "do you remember the day he swam into the river and rescued little Mickileen when the stream was sweeping him away?"

"Why shouldn't I remember it?" answered he. "Yes, Sabby, and you remember the day when I was offered five pounds for him." "Five pounds", she said, turning to me. "Yes, he got five gold sovereigns into the palm of his hand." "My soul! I did" said he, interrupting her, "the bargain was closed and the money in my hand. . . ."

"But", she broke in, "when he saw the poor ass shedding tears because we were parting with him, he couldn't find it in his heart to let him go." "Whist!" said her spouse, "speak gently, I tell you! There isn't a word we're saying that he doesn't understand. See his ear cocked?"

I bid a pound for this marvellous beast.

"A pound", yelled the tramp. "A pound", screamed his wife. "A pound!" roared the twelve children all together.

How astonished they became! They gathered round me to see what I looked like. One urchin took hold of my coat; another of my pants. The youngest of them gripped me round the knee. Another hopeful put her hand into the pocket of my trousers; of course the creature was only trying to find out if I had even the pound, but instead of a pound she got a slap under the ear; and it was not from the tinsman she got it.

* * * * *

I liked the little black ass very well. He would suit my purpose. He would carry me part of my road and I could sell him any time I felt tired of him.

"A pound!" said I again.

"Two pounds", said the tramp.

"O! O!" wailed the woman, "my fine ass going for two pounds", and she broke into sobs and tears.

"For a pound", I insisted.

"For a pound then – and sixpence to each of the children."

The bargain was closed at that. I gave him the pound. I also gave sixpence to each of his children who were ranged around me. The woman had called them up – Seaneen and Nedeen and Taimeen, and I don't know how many others.

There wasn't a beggarman at the fair who didn't bring his offspring about me, all threatening and screaming. What a din they made! What quarrelling and confusion was on every side of me! One complained that he received no sixpence – though the coin was under his tongue at that moment! Another said – but nobody could know what anybody was saying, or trying to say, there was such a hullabaloo.

Pity it was I didn't give him the two pounds at first, and have nothing to do with those presents to his endless family.

I left the village "in state". I was mounted on the ass, the tramp on my right holding the headstall, his wife similarly engaged on my left, the children howling around us.

Some of the village lads followed us, each of them giving me his own bit of advice. The ass was compared to the most famous racehorses of the day.

I was cautioned to be on my guard, lest he might take head and disappear for ever. I was advised to give him such and such a kind of food. One would imagine the crowd had never before seen any object to laugh at, until they beheld me mounted on my little black ass, and escorted along by a band of tramps.

But what cared I? Had I not the ass – just the animal I had been wishing to have for many a day! Can I describe how myself and my ass parted company with this roving escort? Each one of them in succession wrung my hand nine times, and each of them spoke caressingly and coaxingly to the ass . . . His virtues were rehearsed to me, seven times over. A promise was extracted from me that I would be nice and gentle to him, give him a handful of corn whenever I could afford it, give him a wisp of hay at night, and, for the life of me, never, never, use the stick on him. Then, as we were parting, a wail of woe was raised. The father began it. The mother helped him, the children followed suit, until soon the woods around me were filled with their heart-rending lamentations. . . .

I was alone at last – alone with my little black ass.

Off he went at a gallop, until we left the wood behind us. I felt I had made an excellent bargain. Where could anybody find an ass so lively, so spirited, as my little black ass?

But when we had got clear of the wood there was a different story to tell.

A foot he wouldn't stir, this incomparable ass of mine. I thought to coax him along by flattering words. He didn't heed me. I thought to move him with the stick. Stir he would not; but stood fast there in the middle of the road.

People passed by; they had been at the fair and were in merry mood. I was advised to do this, and do that; but when one joker advised me to give the ass a lift on my back, my patience gave out and I threw stones at the ill-natured jester.

At last I had to dismount and drag the ass along against his will. What prayers did I not offer up for the roving rake who had sold me this precious beast!

But soon I observed a peculiar fact. The ass, I could see, was nervous, and the wind playing through the branches of the trees seemed to startle him. As he passed under the arms of the trees that grew by the roadside his laziness at once vanished, and it became almost impossible to hold him in. He would first cock an ear; then he would shake himself as a dog does on leaving the water, and, quick as thought, he would fly ahead like a whirlwind.

I was in luck. I had found out his secret.

I tied him to a gate, went into the wood and plucked an armful of fresh grass and leaves. These I wove into a garland which, as we were leaving the wood, I placed about his neck and over his two ears.

The poor beast! You never saw such speed as he made. He thought because of the music in his ears that he was all the time in the wood. When we arrived at Ballyfeehan all the village turned out to behold the wonder – myself and that little black ass of mine wearing his leafy crown.

* * * * *

I have the little black ass still, and I shall have him until he dies. Many a long mile we have travelled lonely roads in all kinds of weather. He has mended his ways in some respects. His master, alas, has not; and I believe the little black rogue knows as well as anybody in the world that he has not.

But you have never seen anything so proud as he has become of late, since I bought a pretty grey-green car for him. Growing younger the poor creature is ever since I first tackled him to the car.

Pádraic Ó Conaire
Field and Fair 1929

THE CALO DONKEY

We entered the kitchen and sat down at the board, calling for wine and bread. There were two ill-looking fellows in the kitchen smoking cigars. I said something to Antonio in the Calo language.

"What is that I hear?" said one of the fellows, who was distinguished by an immense pair of moustaches – "what is that I hear? Is it in Calo that you are speaking before me, and I a Chalan and National? Accursed gipsy, how dare you enter this posada and speak before me in that speech? Is it not forbidden by the law of the land in which we are, even as it is forbidden for a gipsy to enter the mercado? I tell you what, friend; if I hear another word of Calo come from your mouth, I will cudgel your bones and send you flying over the housetops with a kick of my foot."

"You would do right", said his companion; "the insolence of these gipsies is no longer to be borne. When I am at Merida or at Badajoz I go to the mercado, and there in a corner stand the accursed gipsies jabbering to each other in a speech which I understand not. 'Gipsy gentleman', say I to one of them, 'what will you have for that donkey?' 'I will have ten dollars for it, Caballero Nacional', says the gipsy; 'It is the best donkey in all Spain'. 'I should like to see its paces', say I. 'That you shall, most valorous!' says the gipsy; and jumping upon its back, he puts it to its paces, first of all whispering something into its ear in Calo; and truly the paces of the donkey are most wonderul, such as I have never seen before. 'I think it will just suit me'; and after looking at it awhile, I take out the money and pay for it. 'I shall go to my house', says the gipsy; and off he runs. 'I shall go to my village', say I, and I mount the donkey. 'Vamonos', say I; but the donkey won't move. I give him a switch, but I don't get on the better for that. 'How is this' say I, and I fall to spurring him. What happens then, brother? The wizard no sooner feels the prick than he bucks down and flings me over his head into the mire. I get up and look about me. There stands the donkey staring at me, and there stands the whole gipsy canaille squinting at me with their filmy eyes. 'Where is the scamp who has sold me this piece of furniture?' I shout. 'He is gone to Granada, valorous', says one. 'He is gone to see his kindred among the Moors' says another. 'I just saw him running over the field in the direction of . . . , with the devil close behind him', says a third. In a word, I am tricked. I wish to dispose of the donkey; no one, however, will buy him. He is a Calo donkey, and every person avoids him. At last the gipsies offer thirty rials for him; and after much chaffering I am glad to get rid of him at two dollars. It is all a trick, however: he returns to his master, and the brotherhood share the spoil amongst them."

George Borrow
The Bible in Spain 1843

THE PARAGON

Dear Sir,

I have seen your ad in the Champion today. I got a good ass and I think shes in fole too and she has black ears and whats left on her tale that the ponys after leaving to her bad cess to him is black.

You could say she was a dark ass alright but a bit ruff but if shes ruff shes right too and she has a grand bawl that youd here in America.

Id say she was in fole alright. My missus sais she is and she should know as shes buryed 6 young children God rest there soles and I wasn't there when it happened but she tolt me it was alright.

Shes a aged ass as she was droped the very day my 4th girl was and shes in America this long time but strong.

Don't pay any etenshun to the tinkers mark that does be on her. They done it on me when I had a drink taken.

Im asking £17.10 – seventeen tin for the ass but would take less. Make me an offer.

Hoping you will call, I remain your truly,

(Signed) Tim.

The above is an exact transcription of an original letter sent to Lady Swinfen, author of 'The Irish Donkey'.

ADVICE

"Whatever you do don't give more than half a crown for a donkey. There's no meat on them."

E. O. E. Somerville and Martin Ross
The Experiences of an Irish R.M. 1899

A CRUEL TRICK

I might have travelled about six miles amongst cross roads and lanes, when suddenly I found myself upon a broad and very dusty road which seemed to lead due north. As I wended along this I saw a man upon a donkey riding towards me. The man was commonly dressed, with a broad felt hat on his head and a kind of satchel on his back; he seemed to be in a mighty hurry, and was every now and then belabouring the donkey with a cudgel. The donkey, however, which was a fine large creature of the silver-grey species, did not appear to sympathize at all with its rider in his desire to get on, but kept its head turned back as much as possible, moving from one side of the road to the other and not making much forward way. As I passed, being naturally of a very polite disposition, I gave the man the sele of the day, asking him at the same time why he beat the donkey; whereupon the fellow eyeing me askance, told me to mind my own business, with the addition of something I need not repeat. I had not proceeded a furlong before I saw seated on the dust by the wayside, close by a heap of stones, and with several flints before him, a respectable-looking old man, with a straw hat and a white smock, who was weeping bitterly.

"What are you crying for, father?" said I. "Have you come to any hurt?" "Hurt enough", sobbed the old man, "I have just been tricked out of the best ass in England by a villain, who gave me nothing but these trash in return", pointing to the stones before him. "I really scarcely understand you", said I, "I wish you would explain yourself more clearly". "I was riding on my ass from market", said the old man, "when I met here a fellow with a sack on his back, who, after staring at the ass and me a moment or two, asked me if I would sell her. I told him that I could not think of selling her, as she was very useful to me, and though an animal, my true companion, whom I loved as much as if she were my wife and daughter. I then attempted to pass on, but the fellow stood before me, begging me to sell her, saying that he would give me anything for her; well, seeing that he persisted, I said at last that if I sold her, I must have six pounds for her, and I said so to get rid of him, for I saw that he was a shabby fellow who had probably not six shillings in the world; but I had better have held my tongue", said the old man, crying more bitterly than before, "for the words were scarcely out of my mouth, when he said he would give me what I asked, and taking the sack from his back, he pulled out a steelyard, and going to the heap of stones there, he took up several of them and weighed them, then flinging them down before me, he said, 'There are six pounds, neighbour; now, get off the ass and hand her over to me'. Well, I sat like one dumbfoundered for a time, till at last I asked him what he meant? 'What do I mean?' said he, 'you old rascal, why, I mean to claim my purchase', and then he swore so awfully, that scarcely knowing what I did I got down, and he jumped on the animal and rode off as fast as he could". "I suppose he was the fellow", said I, "whom I just now met upon a fine grey ass, which he was beating with a cudgel". "I dare say he was", said the old man, "I saw him beating her as he rode away, and I thought I should have died." "I never heard such a story", said I; well, do you mean to submit to such a piece of roguery quietly?" "Oh, dear", said the old man, "what can I do? I am seventy-nine years of age; I am bad on my feet, and dar'n't go after him". "Shall I go", said I: "the fellow is a thief, and any one has a right to stop him". "Oh, if you could but bring her to me again", said the old man, "I would bless you till my dying day; but have a care; I don't know but after all the law may say that she is his lawful purchase. I asked six pounds for her, and he gave me six pounds". "Six flints, you mean", said I, "no, no, the law is not quite so bad as that either; I know something about her, and am sure that she will never sanction such a quibble. At all events, I'll ride after the fellow". Thereupon turning my horse round, I put him to his very best trot; I rode nearly a mile without obtaining a glimpse of the fellow, and was becoming apprehensive that he had escaped me by turning down some by-path, two or three of which I had passed. Suddenly, however, on the road making a slight turning, I perceived him right before me, moving at a tolerably swift pace, having by this time probably overcome the resistance of the animal. Putting my horse to a full gallop, I shouted at the top of my voice, "Get off that donkey, you rascal, and give her up to me, or I'll ride you down". The fellow hearing the thunder of the horse's hoofs behind him, drew up on one side of the road. "What do you want?" said he, as I stopped my charger, now almost covered with sweat and foam close beside him. "Do you want to rob me?" "To rob you?" said I. "No! but to take from you that ass, of which you have just robbed its owner." "I have robbed no man", said the fellow; "I just now purchased it fairly of its master, and the law will give it to me; he asked six pounds for it, and I gave him six pounds". "Six stones, you mean, you rascal", said I; "get down, or my horse shall be upon you in a moment"; then with a motion of my reins I caused the horse to rear, pressing his sides with my heels as if I intended to make him leap. "Stop", said the man, "I'll get down and then try if I can't serve you out". He then got down and confronted me with his cudgel; he was a horrible-looking fellow and seemed prepared for anything. Scarcely, however, had he dismounted, when the donkey jerked the bridle out of his hand, and probably in revenge for the usage she had received, gave him a pair of tremendous kicks on the hip with her hinder legs, which overturned him, and then scampered down the road the way she had come. "Pretty treatment this", said the fellow, getting up without his cudgel, and holding his hand to his side, "I wish I may not be lamed for life". "And if you be", said I, "it will merely serve you right, you rascal, for trying to cheat a poor old man out of his property by quibbling at words". "Rascal!" said the fellow, "you lie, I am no rascal; and as for quibbling with words – suppose I did! What then? All the first people does it! The newspapers does it! The gentlefolks that calls themselves the guides of the popular mind does it! I'm no ignoramus. I read the newspapers and knows what's what". "You read them to some purpose", said I. "Well, if you are lamed for life and unfitted for any active line – turn newspaper editor; I should say you are perfectly qualified and this day's adventure may be the foundation of your fortune", thereupon I turned round and rode off. The fellow followed me with a torrent of abuse. "Confound you", said he – yet that was not the expression either – "I know you; you are one of the horse patrol come down into the country on leave to see your relations. Confound you, you and the like of you have knocked my business on the head near Lunnon, and I suppose we shall have you shortly in the country". "To the newspaper office", said I, "and fabricate falsehoods out of the flint stones;" then touching the horse with my heels I trotted off, and coming to the place where I had seen the old man, I found him there, risen from the ground and embracing his ass.

George Borrow
The Romany Rye 1857

THE DONKEY MART

The London Donkey Exchange is the Islington Cattle Market on a Friday afternoon. There some 3,000 "mokes" change hands during a year, the busiest days being the Fridays before and after Bank Holidays, for on these festive occasions there are not a few "donkeys of pleasure" which remain in the same ownership for just seven days, and in that time pay the cost of their purchase and keep and bring the profit on their re-sale.

The biggest of the batches paying toll at Islington come from Ireland. Sometimes a herd of a hundred, sometimes even more, will be met with on the road from Milford or Holyhead, steadily journeying towards the city to which so many hoofs point, and feeding by the wayside as they come; or, and this is the more usual method, crowded in truck-loads on the rail. Not that these big herds are thrown on the market all at once, for the donkey dealer knows his business, and rarely puts in an appearance at Islington with more than a score; the trade is a trade of ones, and twos, and threes, which change owners with much arguing and bargaining, and in which nearly every argument and abatement is emphasised with a more or less affectionate whack on the unfortunate animal's back. The stick-play at a donkey sale is remarkable. "Sure, sir", said one of the bystanders, "the Neddies feel themselves quite at home!"

The track, on the high road, of an Irish donkey drove is easily recognizable owing to the heavy shoes it is the custom to wear in the Emerald Isle – shoes which are promptly replaced by the lighter English pattern as soon as the purchase goes to his new home. Irish are not, however, the heaviest shoes; for those we must go to Egypt, where the native farriers simply cover the feet with a plate. Shoeing a donkey costs sixpence a foot, and the farrier does not "hanker after it." "You see, sir", we heard one of them say, "it's not nearly so easy as a horse; it is a smaller shoe and finer work, and some of the brutes have to be lashed up, and some put on their backs with their feet in the air. However, two shillings is the price for a set, and we cannot raise it, and there's an end of it! Luckily, the shoes last a couple of months!"

We have been assured by a donkey expert that the Irishmen always bray with a brogue, and that without this they would often be unrecognizable; but recent experience has taught us to our sorrow that humorists of the libellous kind are not unkown among donkey drivers. Perhaps our driver had an unusually cultivated ear for vocal music; anyway, after a day's drill we have not found it difficult to identify an Irish donkey nine times out of ten.

There are over 200,000 donkeys in Ireland employed in agriculture, and these are of all sizes, some of the larger having a strain of horse blood in them, as is the case in Italy, where the so-called donkey is a by no means insignificant animal. Italy has more donkeys than any other European country, there being over 700,000 of them there; while France, which of late years has taken to that most difficult of pursuits, mule breeding, has 400,000. The great mule-breeding country is, however, the United States, where there are two and a half millions of mules and donkeys taken together, it being found impossible to separate them owing to the varying proportions of horse ancestry producing an indefinite series from the genuine mule to the asinine mulatto. For the male mule is not always sterile, and the female will breed with horse or ass, or apparently any species of equus.

Next on the list to Ireland, as a source of supply to the London Donkey Market, is "gallant little Wales", whose natives also are credited with a note of their own, shrill, persistent and distressing, though welcome in the owner's ear, for a Welsh donkey is generally a good one; in fact, Wales breeds our best donkeys, and some of them will even fetch as much as 30l.

Donkey breeding has its difficulties, and it does not pay in England. Now that the commons have been inclosed, or taken over by County Councils, and the common rights done away with, pasture for nothing is rarely obtainable, and the margin of profit on a donkey is too small to be worth troubling about. Prices are "up" now, it is true, and a donkey that a few years ago could be had for eighteen shillings will now be cheap at fifty, but the ordinary work-a-day animal does not range much above that price, which we can take as a fair average market rate.

The market has not a thriving look about it. The great area at Islington, with its labyrinth of rails and posts, is all bare except in one corner, and in that about three of the roads are filled, one with donkeys, one with a series of scattered marine stores of harness and horsey sundries, and one with the most miserably weedy ponies and drudges that ever greet the horse-buyer's eye. Here is the tail end of London's horse world, the last refuge of our cheapest beasts of burden, the last chance of the pony, and the first chance of the donkey, brought together so as to show off the donkey to advantage. Great is the clatter as the weedy nags, all heads and legs, are bustled about over the stones, with a whip here and a whip there to make them swerve and scamper as they are shown off before the "nibbler". "We call 'em nibblers, sir, 'cos they don't always bite!" There is a refreshing candour about the whole affair which effectually disarms criticism. "He ain't much to look at, mister, but then I don't ask much. He might suit you at the price. Four pun ten ain't much for a oss!"

"Try a donkey, sir?" Well, one would rather. A good donkey is a better servant than a bad horse. In proportion to his size he will bear a heavier burden and drag a greater weight. He will eat not a quarter of what a horse does, and he will live at least twice as long. "How long will a donkey live?" we asked Mr. Gill of Hampstead. "Live? Well, I know one that has lived thirty-seven years and seen three generations of the family from babhood to babhood!"

And what becomes of the dead donkeys? A good many go in their last days to this Mr. Gill, who supplies them wholesale to the Veterinary College for dissecting purposes, the anatomy of the donkey being almost identical with that of the horse – in fact, a donkey is practically a horse, minus the callosities on the hind legs, and plus the tufted tail and long ears.

The dead or moribund horse goes to the knackers, "the practical zootomists", as they are beginning to call themselves, but the knacker will rarely have anything to do with the donkey, which is hardly worth the cost of carriage. Five shillings is his outside value for his hoofs, his bones and skin – chiefly his skin, out of which we get shagreen leather and memorandum tablets, and perhaps a drumhead or two, though drumheads are nowadays mostly made of Canadian deerskin. The flesh is worthless. It is only the Persian who will eat ass's flesh, and even he must have it wild, after hunting it, as if asses were deer. . . .

The donkey of our streets is a better animal than he used to be. He is bigger and healthier, he is fed better, and he does more work. The work done by these donkeys is remarkable; I have known one in the shafts of a South London milk-cart which for eight months travelled 140 miles a week in doing the daily round.

Some of this improvement is certainly due to the shows, the chief of which is the triennial one, which now sometimes holds its meeting at the People's Palace. A queer show is this, for not only do the donkeys come, but they have to bring with them their barrows all duly loaded up with vegetables, or fish, or firewood, or whatever it may be, out of which the "commercial traveller", as the costermonger now calls himself, earns his living. Of course every donkey has a name, such a name as one would give to a horse – many of the names such as are borne by winning race-horses. Some of the donkeys have been working for their owners seven, ten or fifteen years; some of them are even entered as twenty years old; and in most cases, without a rest, they have worked their six days a week, year in, year out. Every donkey has his price, often as fictitious as that given at a bird show, but occasionally genuine and such as would lead to business, even though it may be 15l. or 20l. or 30l. Even at Islington these high-priced animals are to be met with, but not in the pens; they are in the light carts and barrows of the donkey dealers, who would think it *infra dig.* to drive a pony. Some of these thoroughbreds have pedigrees going back for several generations and the starting of a Donkey Stud Book is evidently an event of the near future.

Away from the crowd, in a pen by themselves, harnessed up to their traps and with cloths over them, we find two of these aristocrats admirably groomed and in the pink of condition. The cloth is taken off one that we may inspect her. "That is White Jenny. She'll do her six miles inside thirty minutes any day you please!" "And the other?" "The Skewbald? He is as good." "And what is Jenny worth?" "Forty-five pounds, not a penny less!" "But is that not rather a long price?" "Maybe, but she's good. What is a good horse worth compared to a bad one? How do you know a good horse from a bad one? By opinion. And that is how we know a good donkey from a bad one. That is not the highest price asked for a donkey. Why, I know a pair that changed hands for a hundred and twenty pounds – yes, one hundred and twenty; sixty pounds apiece!"

And yet such scope is there for opinion that the rates at which the lots are being parted for in the market do not average as many shillings. This is for "Jacks" for ordinary driving among costers and organ-men. But we are here reminded that there is a curious by-way of the donkey world concerning itself with "milch asses". These have been bought for 12l., but they generally range from 7l. to 8l., being sold again after six months at from 2l. to 3l. Asses' milk was at one time a favourite with physicians. Being more sugary and less cheesy than that of the cow, it was well suited for weaklings and invalids of a consumptive turn, and a fairly large business was done in it. But the patent foods came in with their voluminous advertisements, and the trade has almost died out. It is most in evidence in one or two of the West End squares during the season, where a donkey, with a goat in the cart, may be seen in the morning going round to be milked. If there are fifty milch asses in London it is as much as there are, the oldest firm at work being that of Dawkins, of Bolsover Street, which has been selling asses' milk ever since 1780, and, what is more extraordinary, jobbing out milch asses to families, sending them far and wide into the country, accompanied with full printed directions as to how to milk and treat them. As an ass will yield about a quart a day, the London supply could easily be got into a single churn, and is manifestly microscopic, but the jobbing is not so insignificant a business, and is certainly worth a note.

Donkey jobbing in its draught and riding branches exists, but does not flourish. Here and there one hears of men with studs ranging up to fifty, but they are not numerous. Ten is the average stud of the donkey master, and there are about five hundred donkeys thus "standing at livery". It is not a satisfactory business to run, and many people have burnt their fingers at it.

A donkey out on hire for a month is at the mercy of his hirer, who is not always merciful, and it is frequently returned so over-driven and knocked about that it takes two months to return to decent condition; and as the charge for hire is three shillings a week, the twelve shillings spread over three months is not much to get a living out of, although it may mean 75 per cent per annum on the capital invested. The poor willingly pay high percentages, owing to the amounts they deal with being so trifling. The same rule holds good in all trades; on a large return a living is possible on a small percentage, but where the return is small the percentage must be large. No wonder, then, that to hire a donkey many a costermonger has to borrow the money at 20 per cent per week.

Many of the donkeys at the Islington market appear there two or three times during the year, and all the 3,000 are not used up in London, for Brighton and Margate and other seaside pleasure towns are supplied from the London centre. Against this we must put the private sales, for many of our donkeys change hands without visiting Islington. Altogether there seem to be about thirteen thousand donkeys in the county of London. These mostly begin work at two years old, though they ought not to begin until they are four, and they are very seldom used for riding purposes until they have turned three.

But the riding donkeys are few in number. On recent application to the County Council, we were officially informed that only fifty-seven drivers now hold licences to let out donkeys on the open spaces under the Council's control, and that each licence only entitles the holder to let out five animals. . . .

Those who would see the coster's donkey at his best should go to Billingsgate or the vegetable markets early in the morning. There they will find him smartened up by his drive from home, and contentedly waiting for his load; and they will probably be astonished at his being on the whole so cheery and well. Donkeys on hire are often ill-treated, but a donkey driven by his owner is generally looked after kindly, inasmuch as few men care to damage their own property. Many of these costers' donkeys come pattering along with a briskness and assurance that can only come of contentment with their work, and some of the smallest even are as active and "packed with power" as one could wish, and with a quiet, fearless outlook, speaking volumes for their master. Here and there some exceptionally good-looking examples will be pointed out to a newcomer as "known in the shows" or "on the road", and hoping to be better known, perhaps next year in the Donkey Derby which is being organized by Mr. John Atkinson, the well-known medical superintendent of the Animals' Institute in Wilton Place; the idea of the competition being that racing will improve the breed by encouraging emulation among the breeders. . . .

Drawing by Leesa Sandys-Lumsdaine

Costers' donkeys are not generally tended in sitting-rooms, though their stable accommodation is peculiarly varied. A shed or a lean-to against the back-yard wall seems to be the prevailing fashion, with the cart alongside and the harness indoors; for the harness may be worth as much as the cart or the donkey. A good set will cost 7l., a bad one may be had for as many pence, there being a lower depth in rag and rope than that displayed in the marine stores on the Islington stones, where the line seems to be drawn at the old carriage harness, which makes the poor little donkey look like a street Arab in a man's coat.

Miserable as many of these turn-outs may look – animal, harness and vehicle complete – it will be found that they "bulk into money". There are 7,500l. worth of donkeys alone changing hands at the London mart during the year, and the carts are worth quite as much as the power that draws them. The costermonger begins business with a basket; from that he advances to a hand-truck; and from that, when he has amassed sufficient capital, he rises to the dignity of the donkey-cart, which made its first appearance amongst us in the days of Elizabeth, when donkeys first became common in these islands . . . .

It may seem a mystery why the donkey market should be held in such an unexpected place. Of course, it went there from Smithfield with the cattle market. But why did it begin at Smithfield? For the same reason as the cattle market did; because the animals could be conveniently watered at the old Horse Pool, which once lay between the moor fields and the smooth field that served the citizens as a playground. And the Friday market on that field was at least as old as the days of Fitzstephen, and even in those days it included the draught animals and "peasants' wares" we find represented today among the posts and rails of Islington.

W. J. Gordon
The Horse World of London 1893

"AT SMITHFIELD RACES"

When a costermonger wishes to see or buy a donkey, he goes to Smithfield market on a Friday afternoon. On this day, between the hours of one and five there is a kind of fair held, attended solely by costermongers, for whose convenience a long paved slip of ground, about eighty feet in length, has been set apart. The animals for sale are trotted up and down this – the "racecourse", as it is called – and on each side of it stand the spectators and purchasers, crowding among the stalls of peas-soup, hot eels and other street delicacies.

Everything necessary for the starting of a costermonger's barrow can be had in Smithfield on a Friday – from the barrow itself to the weights – from the donkey to the whip. The animals can be purchased at prices ranging from 5s. to 3l. On a brisk market-day as many as two hundred donkeys have been sold. The barrows for sale are kept apart from the steeds, but harness to any amount can be found everywhere, in all degrees of excellence, from the bright japanned cart saddle with its new red pads, to the old mouldy trace covered with buckle marks. Wheels of every size and colour, and springs in every stage of rust, are hawked about on all sides. To the usual noise and shouting of a Saturday night's market is added the shrill squeal of distant pigs, the lowing of the passing oxen, the bleating of sheep and the braying of donkeys. The paved road all down the "race-course" is level and soft, with the mud trodden down between the stones. The policeman on duty there wears huge fisherman's or flushermen's boots, reaching to their thighs, and the trouser ends of the costers' corduroys are black and sodden with wet dirt. Every variety of odour fills the air; you pass from the stable smell that hangs about the donkeys, into an atmosphere of apples and fried fish, near the eating stalls, while a few paces further on you are nearly choked with the strench of goats. The crowd of black hats, thickly dotted with red and yellow plush caps, reels about; and the "hi-hi-i-i" of the donkey runners sounds on all sides. Sometimes a curly-headed bull, with a fierce red eye, on its way to or from the adjacent cattle-market, comes trotting down the road, making all the visitors rush suddenly to the railings, for fear – as a coster near me said – of "being taught the hornpipe".

The donkeys standing for sale are ranged in a long line on both sides of the "race-course", their white velvety noses resting on the wooden rail they are tied to. Many of them wear their blinkers and head harness, and others are ornamented with ribbons, fastened in their halters. The lookers-on lean against this railing and chat with the boys at the donkeys' heads, or with the men who stand behind them, and keep continually hitting and shouting at the poor still beasts to make them prance. Sometimes a party of two or three will be seen closely examining one of these "Jerusalem ponys", passing their hands down its legs, or looking quietly on, while the proprietor's ash stick descends on the patient brute's back, making a dull hollow sound. As you walk in front of the long line of donkeys, the lads seize the animals by their nostrils and show their large teeth, asking if you "want a hass, sir", and all warranting the creature to be "five years old next buff-day". Dealers are quarrelling among themselves, downcrying each other's goods. "A hearty man", shouted one proprietor, pointing to his rival's stock, "could eat three sich donkeys as yourn at a meal".

One fellow, standing behind his steed, shouts as he strikes, "Here's the real Britannia mettle"; whilst another asks "Who's for the Pride of the Market?" and then proceeds to flip "the pride" with his whip till she clears away the mob with her kickings. Here, standing by its mother, will be a shaggy little colt, with a group of ragged boys fondling it and lifting it in their arms from the ground.

During all this the shouts of the drivers and runners fill the air as they rush past each other on the race-course. Now a tall fellow, dragging a donkey after him, runs by crying as he charges in amongst the mob, "Hulloa! Hulloa! hi! hi!", his mate, with his long coat-tails flying in the wind, hurrying after and roaring, between his blows, "Keem-up!"

Henry Mayhew
Mayhew's London 1851

STUD ADVERTISEMENT FOR: "THE OLD KNIGHT OF MALTA"

Imported by General Washington, from the Island of Malta, and undoubtedly the finest Jack upon the Continent, will stand at the White House, in New Kent county, on the River Pamonkey, the seat of George Washington P. Custis, Esq.* and be let to mares at EIGHT DOLLARS the season, and half a dollar to the groom, provided a sufficient subscription can be obtained by the first of March.

The merits of the animal are too well-known to need any illustration. The advantages resulting from the use of Mules in an agricultural point of view, must be obvious to every person acquainted in that line. Subscriptions will be received (specifying the number of Mules or Jennetts) by Mr. William BOOKER, Union Tavern, Richmond and the subscriber, WILLIAM STUART, Agent for the Estate of

George W. P. Custis, Esq.
at White House, New Kent. Feb 2, 1802

---

*George Washington P. Custis was General Washington's grandson

PRICES IN POITOU

Some idea of the scale and economic importance of Poitevin ass-breeding in its heyday at the end of the nineteenth century may be formed from the report made by Charles L. Sutherland to the Richmond Commission on Agriculture:

> The Poitevin jackass, a variety as curious and perhaps as ugly as he is massive, short-legged and valuable, . . . is the most important of all quadrupeds in Poitou. He is the sire of the mules, and as such is the direct means of putting large sums of money into the pockets of the farmers. The price of a young improved animal of two years varies from £80 to £120; a good proved mule-getter, four year old, from 14 to 15 hands high, is worth from £200 to £320, and one was sold in the Vendée, just before the Franco-Prussian war, for £400. These valuable animals are kept in a filthy state, are never groomed, and never taken out of the building in which they are kept, except to be shown to a visitor or possible purchaser. The fee for the service of each mare is from 16s. to 20s. The female asses are rarely parted with, except for some defect. Their value may be set down at £24 to £40. The Conseil General of the Deux-Sèvres vote annually the sum of £200 for prizes for mules and asses at the local shows. These establishments are technically called *ateliers*, and the fact of owning such an establishment entitles the proprietor to the right to call himself *maître*, and gives him a position in the country. Each stud farm consists of from four to seven stallion asses, a stallion horse, a "teaser", and one or more she-asses. The mares are also brought to the stud-farms, of which there are 160 in Poitou, the Deux-Sèvres alone claiming 94, with 465 jackasses. The resultant males were sold at three or four years old, in the early months of the year, at fairs attended by dealers from all over the South of France, from Spain, and from Italy; good ones fetched £60 to £80, inferior ones half that sum. We must leave the reader to translate the quotations in late Victorian pounds into terms of whatever purchasing-power sterling may have on the date when this work comes from the press. But even now, the top price of £400 quoted above represents, certainly, more than £1000 in contemporary currency.

Anthony Dent
Donkey: The Story of the Ass from East to West 1972

DONKEY WORK

When I lived in Stepney, almost opposite the then new People's Palace, there were a lot of donkeys in the East End. The rows of country-type cottages had little shut-in gardens at their backs and the costers' donkeys lived there, behind the cottages, and you could watch them in the morning coming out through the front doors; picking their way, neat-footed, over the babies playing on the doorstep, or down the narrow passage.

Every coster owned a donkey, as one of the family, and those I knew were well cared for. The costers' barrows and carts could be piled up in yards, but

when released, each donkey trotted off to his home, and if the door was ajar, he'd shove it open and walk in. They were very sociable and reliable donkeys.

I remember the doctor who lived down there: he decided he'd get a donkey and trap, to be at the country station to meet him and take his bags and books up to his weekend home. Well the trap was easy; he'd only to choose one for himself, but when he asked a local patient friend for a "recommended moke" the matter was taken out of his hands. A perfect Board Meeting of Experts took over, and selecting "the doctor's donkey" took all of three weeks (and pints of lubrication).

At last, one Sunday, he was called out. The entire costers' committee had

lined up eight donkeys on parade in the street outside. They were a lovely lot. Coats brushed to gloss, and oiled hoofs and little shoes shined bright as silver. All stood in a neat row, nose to pavement – the very cream of Stepney donkeys.

He was told he "couldn't go wrong with any of them" – but it took all morning. Every single donkey was trotted up and down to show off his paces; teeth were examined; ears flapped; and each foot lifted in turn till – at last – the donkey was chosen and "they reckoned the doctor had got what he ought to have."

So – donkey and trap went off to Hampshire and were duly met at the local station and loaded up and jingled away – exactly as far as the station lights lasted. But not an inch into the dark night beyond. In vain the spanky new candle lamps flickered behind his ears – in vain coercion. No proper town-bred donkey would face the utter dark beyond the station lamps. It just was not done. No moke bred in the well-lit Commercial Road would do it. Not till a large stable lantern was carried ahead, and his reassuring owner walked with him, did that donkey, obedient but apprehensive, venture, trembling, over the four miles home to his new stable (and then they had to leave the light burning and install a friendly cat before he would go to bed). Very set in their ways are Londoners.

That was years ago, before the one way traffic and roundabouts came into use. Piccadilly Circus was one of the first places to have regulated traffic enforced. The police arrived at 5 a.m. – for the early Covent Garden Market traffic, and the lorries and heavy dray carts jibbed a bit, and a few late night revellers' cabs resented it, but the costers' donkeys just rebelled: they lay down and flatly refused to go the wrong way round. They had trotted up to Market one way for generations. They knew which was the right way – the way they had always gone. As rebellion spread, chaos of cluttered carts blocked the streets till in desperation the arm of the law gave way. It was several mornings before the Stepney donkeys accepted the strange ruling.

Dorothy Hartley
The Guardian

PETRONELLA

I stood in the dusty pound at Lydenburg, South Africa, and watched the unwanted donkeys being put up for sale. Most of the unfortunate animals were sold, and I didn't like the way their new owners took possession, thrashing their purchases before ever a task was set them and their willingness tested. One by one, and in small groups, the little pilgrims were set on the dreary road that leads through labour and starvation to merciful death.

At last there was only one left, an old grey jenny with one eye blinded and one torn ear hanging loppily from its middle. She was covered with ticks, her knees were bent and her head hung down. A picture of dejection.

A young native bid sixpence for her and laughed raucously. I was prospecting for gold at the time and almost down but not out, for I still had my tools and six shillings in cash. I had intended buying a bag of meal and supplementing my sugar and coffee supply. But now I knew that I must buy the aged jenny and sacrifice a precious cartridge as well. Between the eyes and a little above, and she'd never know what hit her.

I raised the bidding to a shilling and watched my extra coffee go down the drain. The other fellow bid one and three. I sent my sugar ration after the coffee and upped it threepence more. My opponent made a scornful remark and slouched off; the donkey was mine to release through the barrel of my old Smith and Wesson, as soon as we could get out of town. For no reason at all I named her Petronella.

Getting her out of town wasn't going to be easy, by the look of her, so I dug into my pack for some salt, which is ambrosia to asses the world over. Her good ear pricked up as I held the dainty under her muzzle. Her nose wrinkled ecstatically as she crunched it, and she emitted those curious death-rattlelike sounds which in the asinine etiquette indicate pleasure. With more salt on my palm, I led her away and up the road.

It is bad manners to carry a gun in town, so the old Smith and Wesson was in my pack. When we came to a sufficiently remote spot I transferred its holster to my belt.

The action reminded Petronella of goodies and she edged nearer ingratiatingly. I gave her a little salt and then, for some quite inexplicable reason, I fastened my pack on her emaciated back. She pricked her good ear forward and started off up the mountain trail in front of me as a well-trained pack animal should. Gone was the air of dejection, and gone too, the bent and trembling knee. In place of the sorry moke in the pound was a frail but determined old lady, loved and ready to get back to the sort of task she understood. She brought a curious kind of dignity to her labour.

I thought: "Well, if she gives me any trouble or looks like falling, I'll bump her off, but it's nice not having to carry the pack." Even then I knew I could no more shoot Petronella than fly.

She gave me trouble all right. The very first night she chewed my pack about, trying to get at the salt inside. The next night, after we had made camp, she disappeared. I thought: "Good riddance", but then I started worrying in case she had broken a leg, or a snake had bitten her, and so I spent half the night searching. When I finally gave up and returned, she was lying next to the ashes of my fire, chewing away at the pack once more. After that I stopped worrying, and in the year during which she and I fossicked around she often went off on her own for a few hours, but always came back in time to carry her load.

She invented a little game after she felt she knew me well enough to take liberties. Whenever we approached a spinney where the bush was thick, she would gallop ahead and hide in it. Having found the sort of cover she needed to fool me, she would stand dead still while I fumed and fretted, usually within a couple of yards of her hide-out. After half an hour of this kind of fun she would bray derisively, to show me where she had been all the time, and then trot up and nuzzle at my pockets, demanding a reward for being so darned clever.

Those were halcyon days, for our needs were small and the country supplied most of them. Long, hot days and clear, cool nights, rain sometimes but always followed by the drying-out sun and wind. We knew thirst, too, but never badly, for Petronella's instinct was infallible and all I had to do was give her her head and follow her lean little rump to a water hole.

One day an old fellow turned up with a whole string of donkeys, and one of them was a jack. Petronella should have known better, at her age. But girls will be girls, and in due course the horrible truth became obvious – Petronella was about to become a mother.

When her time was near, I had to go into Lydenburg on urgent business and so I left her in charge of a boy I thought I could trust. I returned inside a week, late at night and during a terrific storm. I went to look for my boy to find out how Petronella fared. He had disappeared, and so had most of my kit. I stumbled about in the mud and rain, waiting for flashes of lightning to show me where the jenny was. And then I heard the jackals yip-yapping and snarling on a plateau above the spring.

I got there just too late, for the brutes had torn at the little body of the foal as it was born, and it died as I lifted it up. Petronella had fought them off for as long as she was able. She was in a terrible state, her muzzle ripped and her flank savaged. Carrying the dead foal I led her back to the shack and bedded her down where I had light to see to dress her wounds.

All next day she followed me about like a dog, and when I stopped she

'Donkey and Foal' by Terence Cuneo

pressed her head against my thigh, her misery too much to bear alone. She would not eat or drink, and her one fear seemed to be that I would go away and leave her again. She died on the evening of the second day after my return, with her maimed ear pressed against my side and her poor, thin flank heaving less and less, until it finally went quite flat and was still.

I dug a deep hole where no gold would ever be found and cheated the jackals by laying heavy rocks over her body and over the closed grave as well. I buried the child of her dotage with her.

As I did so I remembered the black cross etched over her withers, the beam straight down her spine and the bar crucifix from side to side. Coloured servants in the Cape used to tell us, long ago, that the mark was imprinted on the hides of grey donkeys because once The Man rode one in triumphant humility before mankind.

A. G. McRae
The Johannesburg Star 1950

6. Donkey Doctrines and Dictums

A IS FOR ASS

The Absolutely Abstemious Ass,
who resided in a Barrel, and only lived on
Soda Water and Pickled Cucumbers.

Edward Lear
Six Nonsense Alphabets 1889

"YOU ASS"

I had long wondered how the word ass ever came to be applied to human beings as an epithet for stupidity. Stubborn as a donkey often is, but very rarely stupid, unless it is stupid to like thistles. Stubborn, slow, detached, but always with some purpose between those ears, always aware of what is going on; whereas when we say, "Don't be such an ass", we mean "Don't be so foolish", "Don't be so feather-brained", "Pull yourself together." And when it comes to obstinacy, we forget the donkey altogether and resort to his cousin the mule. "Don't be such a mule", "Don't be so mulish."

My acquaintance with donkeys has not been large, but such as I have known have been typical. The first was many years ago at Littlehampton; the donkey on which I had my first ride, on a very painful saddle fastened over a light-brown Holland caparison. If it is stupid to wish on a hot summer day, to take things easy, this creature was far from wise. If it is stupid wanting to get back a little of one's own, to rub one's rider's legs against a post, this animal was totally lacking in sagacity. He was stupid too in having four legs and a subservient status and no soul, thus qualifying to be the property of a bullying bi-pedal owner; but otherwise I should call him clever enough, and it certainly was not because of him that I fell into the common habit of saying to other boys, "Don't be such an ass."

That was my first donkey and a certain number of faithful and strongly individualized Neddies followed, all doing their own work in their own watchful way, and all gradually winning respect if not affection. And none of them stupid. And then came, the other day, my latest contact with this cautious friend of man, when, in North Africa, I found him in his thousands, usually very much smaller than we see him in England but working very much harder. No one, for instance, has ever seen a costermonger riding his donkey; at the most he perches on his barrow and urges the little hoofs along, and along they go, apparently quite happily. But it is a common thing to see two full-sized Arabs seated gravely on a donkey so tiny they could easily carry it under the arm. To be so small and bear so much, partakes no doubt, of what

might be called stupidity of a kind; but we must discriminate. Acceptance of *force majeure* should not be thus described.

I am not sure that the real ass is not the camel, because the camel is big enough to be able to resist and do damage. But we never say "Don't be such a camel", at least not in England, although a Paris taxi-driver who deemed himself underpaid once called me an éspèce of one.

Now and then the Algerian donkey has a chance of retaliating and takes it. I shall never forget the satisfaction with which a mother donkey and its most ingratiating offspring, the gayest, naughtiest little thing you ever imagined, held up our car for some minutes while they rolled on their backs in the middle of the road. Stupid? Foolish? Not the terms I should use.

So much for the donkeys of fact. When it comes to such donkeys of fiction as I can recall there is again no question of foolishness. Stevenson's Modestine was not foolish; she was sympathetic. Eeyore may not be an encyclopedia, but he is simple, naive and quick to comment on the lack of brains in others: in fact anything but an ass.

Is it possible, I ask myself, that when one donkey wishes to reprimand or caution another donkey he says, "Don't be such a man?"

E. V. Lucas
Punch 1935

JUDGING DONKEYS, 1968

How to judge a donkey? That question is often being thrown at me and not without some levity. But with nearly 100 shows this year from as far afield, and as illustrious, as the Royal Highland to the Royal Windsor, and all including donkey classes in their schedules, a serious answer is required.

The Donkey Show Society [now the Donkey Breed Society], has established a Judges Panel and has selected, in nearly every case, men and women who are already accredited horse and pony judges, or who have had practical and long experience with horses and ponies. This fact has raised some queries, but as the donkey shares membership of the *genus equus* with the horse I maintain a sound pony judge should make a better attempt at assessing the qualities of a donkey than a judge of cats or budgerigars. There are certainly nothing like enough people available possessing lifelong experience with donkeys to tackle the job.

What should the donkey judge look for? The answer is an animal of balanced proportions and one which, within its inherent limitations, possesses many of the characteristics of a good pony. Of course there are different types of donkeys, four sizes being officially recognized: Miniatures, Small Standards, Standards, Large Standards.

Whatever the size, the fundamental characteristics remain the same. The perceptive judge prefers a small head, and here conformation varies enormously, for often a good donkey is marred by a long, heavy head, while others possess the esteemed, neat, dished profile reminiscent of a well-bred Jersey cow. When I was a child many ponies, other than show exhibits, inherited big coarse heads. Today this fault, because of intelligent selective breeding has virtually disappeared and the same could happen in the donkey world. We should look, therefore, for small quality heads with ears set low and wide apart.

The neck should have length with no evidence of "ewe" concavity, and it should join symmetrically into the body. It is no good expecting the donkey to show any withers – they are non-existent and for this reason the line of the back should be level, though a brood mare may be excused a slight dip. Where to put the saddle? A crupper provides the only guarantee of keeping it in the right place, for donkey shoulders are rather straight. Some, of course, are straighter than others, a point which judges must consider, for it is the oblique which provides the better movement.

A donkey must be strong and sturdy but never coarse. The chest, therefore, should show some width and heart room, the ribs be well sprung, and, above all, there should be no slackness in the loins. It is behind the saddle that donkeys most frequently collect serious faults; weak quarters are also often evident. Really faulty conformation cannot be altered, but long reining can do much to build up muscle.

Legs must be considered in relation to the size of the animal – a large standard needs good bone to carry the body. Little is known about the density of asinine bone and research is now in hand on this important point. The knees in every case must be flat and wide, the hocks set low, and the shorter the cannon bones the better – all points which we require in a good pony. The donkey hind leg, however, often tends to be either sickle or cow-hocked, both serious faults that only careful selective breeding over the years can eliminate. "Donkey feet" is a derogatory term in the pony world, but here we look for the typical neat steep-sided hoof of the donkey species. Low heels of course are deprecated and regular trimming of the hoof is essential.

The improvement in donkey feet at the various shows has been remarkable, but the real sensation has been in donkey action. Given the opportunity donkeys can, and should, move well, straight and without "plaiting" or going too close behind. They will school surprisingly easily to trot out smartly for the judge's appraisal, and good free action can send a donkey up several places in a class. Leaders seem to have achieved the necessary expertise with encouraging results and an obstinate animal is now the exception.

Does a judge like to see donkeys clipped out, trimmed and with plaited manes? There is no official ruling on these points, but personally I like donkeys presented in the same manner as our mountain and moorland ponies – beautifully clean and well-groomed but otherwise *au naturel* unless perhaps some mishap dictates otherwise. I remember a mane which had been chewed by a goat looking much better with plaits!

And what about colour? Broken coated (skewbald or piebald) and pink, or what I designate as strawberry roan, have become modish. There are also dark brown donkeys, milk white donkeys; some grow a 4 in. long coat and never cast it even in the summer, but like horses and ponies a good donkey can never be a bad colour and, of course, is judged on conformation and action, not on permutations of shading.

But most important of all, the judge must look for that vital quality – true donkey character – and we are not talking of that false image of obstinacy, but of the kind, friendly temperament and lovable appeal that more than anything else explains the rocketing popularity of the humble ass of today.

Stella A. Walker
The Field 1968

Grove Hill Stud's 'Menier' at Hambledon Hunt Show

CALCULATING THE WEIGHT OF A DONKEY

If the measurement of the donkey's girth in inches = a, and the length of the donkey's back, from the *top* of its tail to the *base* of its neck (its withers) in inches = b

$$\frac{a^2 \times b}{300} = \text{the donkey's weight in lbs.}$$

The Donkey Show Society Magazine

A DONKEY'S SOLILOQUY

Till now we've been beasts of burden
And had to work hard for our living
But we've been, God wot, quite content with our lot
And our labours of doing and giving.

We've always been ready and willing
To do all that our masters could ask
Tho', loaded and harried, the burdens we carried
Were more like an elephant's task.

But now all that seems to be changing
Like the phantasies seen in a dream,
Our lives undergo rearranging
And we're rising in human esteem.

We now find ourselves petted and pampered,
Of food we have more than our fill,
No more are we harnessed or hampered
And we're suffered to wander at will.

Donkeys, it seems are in fashion;
They win prizes at rallies and shows
(They can also win plenty of cash on
The side, as the cute owner knows).

It's all mighty fine for us donkeys
But, to quote a Darwinian text,
These humans are very like monkeys
And you never know what they'll do next!

H. Stuart Hogg
Donkey Breed Society Magazine 1970

TRAINING TRICKS AND TRAITS

Rules are made to be broken! There comes a stage in your relationship with your donkey, when you can do the most outrageous things, and yet no harm will result. In fact, doing outrageous things can actually be a part of your training programme, *once you have got the full confidence of your donkey.* Some child is going to be unable to resist the temptation to pull his tail, and to lark about around his heels, inviting a kick. So do all you can to make him kick-proof, and accustom him to the things which a child might do. Throw coats over his back and neck. Kick things about the ground. Drop stable brooms. Drag things along the ground, around him. There is no end to the number of "scare-tests" you can think up.

My donkeys are pretty shock-proof on the whole; but there was one occasion which proved too much for them. I was about to walk two donks up the ramp of a box, when the driver, in a moment of lunacy, hurled out a large piece of carpet with which he had intended to cover the rump struts . . . It landed on our heads, and the next thing I knew was that the donks and I were fifty yards down the drive in considerable disarray. It was not the best of things to have happened at that particular moment. Why it did not put an end to the donks boxing with ease, for all time, I shall never understand.

Of course, as a general rule, you would never chase animals in a field. Yet, with reference to the opening sentence of this chapter, the time may come when you can do this deliberately, with impunity! Donkeys love to play. Mine "tell" me when they want a game in the paddock. My part of the game is easy. I only have to pretend to be a bogey, and make as if to chase them. I crouch down, raise my arms, walk in an odd manner, and assume a bogey voice. This is enough for the donks, who, pretending to be scared out of their wits, go galloping off in a big circle; only to veer in towards me to be "frightened" all over again. They "laugh" by holding their noses high whilst running, and turning their faces from side to side. The delightful thing about this game is that it can be stopped as easily as it is started, just by telling the donks that it is over. Then they will come up to be made a fuss of; or caught, if one so wishes. They are a little breathless and excited, and seem to say "We *knew* it was you all the time, really!" You need to be very sure of your donk before playing games like this, or you may find that you are making a good job of training it to be uncatchable!

Animal training is a combination of common sense, and a "feel" for the procedure. Some people are born with the "feel"; others can acquire it to a large degree from tuition and experience. Above all, it should be enjoyable! For both the trainer and the animal. Often, it is far from so. Certain factors turn the whole thing into a battle. The old "Time is Money" evil. Lack of

imagination on the part of the trainer. Extraordinary demands being made upon the animal; "success" being achieved by the belief that the end justifies the means (the ultimate end often being money). One hears it pronounced that animals cannot be trained by cruelty. This is not true. One can debate the word "cruelty" almost endlessly. I use it in its averagely commonsense interpretation. Obviously one must have the upper hand in animal training; but one should aim for total co-operation as opposed to total domination. When a person sets out to "master" an animal, something unpleasant creeps in. The process of producing a brain-washed and utterly broken animal is even more degrading for the trainer than for the animal; though the trainer is often unaware of this, his or her make-up being lavishly supplied with insensitivity. Their physiognomy betrays them every time.

The normal demands made upon the donkey are, happily, very simple and entirely within the range of its high intelligence. If your donk appears to be coming half way to meet you in what you ask of it, and is clearly pleased with itself when it does well, then your training is progressing on the right lines.

Marjorie Dunkels
Training Your Donkey 1970

Do not call your brother an ass for you are the next of kin.

Maltese Proverb

Better to ride on an ass that carries me than on a horse that throws me.

George Herbert
Outlandish Proverbs 1640

An ass is but an ass though laden with gold.

17th century Proverb

Asses as well as pitchers have ears.

Proverb

FAITH

FIRST PART

I had a donkey
Took it to a Show.
Would it trot when I asked?
Oh dear no!

Did the little perisher
Do it out of spite?
After all, it trotted
At *home* alright!

At Shows it went peculiar,
And wouldn't be led.
"What's wrong?" I hissed at it,
And it said:

"Pardon me! I thought
You thought I wouldn't
Then I felt peculiar
And found that I *couldn't*!

Next time if I have
Your faith and trust
I will trot for you
Until I bust!"

SECOND PART

I took my donkey
To another Show,
Thinking and *believing*
It would go.

It went like a bomb!
Just as it should!
And why not, pray? –
When I *knew* that it would!

Gone were the doubts
And the moments of stress –
Would it trot past the Judge!
Yes, yes, YES!

Let all us Owners
Take a vow today
Not to cause our donkeys
To turn round and say

"Pardon me! I thought
You thought I wouldn't!
Then I felt peculiar
And found that I *couldn't*!"

Marjorie Dunkels
Training Your Donkey 1970

A FABLE

(*in imitation of Dryden*)
A dingy donkey, formal and unchanged,
Browsed in the lane and o'er the common ranged.
Proud of his ancient asinine possessions,
Free from the panniers of the grave professions,
He lived at ease; and chancing once to find
A lion's skin, the fancy took his mind
To personate the monarch of the wood;
And for a time the stratagem held good
He moved with so majestical a pace
That bears and wolves and all the savage race
Gazed in admiring awe, ranging aloof.
Not over-anxious for a clearer proof –
Longer he might have triumphed – but alas'
In an unguarded hour it came to pass
He bray'd aloud; and showed himself an ass!

J. H. Frere

THE OLD LION

The Lion, once of forests king,
Now old and mourning his dead past,
By former subjects was at last
Assailed, strong by his weakening.
The Horse, approaching, kicked him sore;
He felt the Wolf's tooth, the Bull's horn;
And languishing, morose, forlorn,
Crippled by age, could hardly roar.
Patient he waited his last breath,
Till e'en the Ass drew near his cave
Then cries aloud – Death I could brave;
To feel thy kicks is more than death.

Jean de la Fontaine
Fables 1668
Translated by Phosphor Mallam

TIT FOR TAT

John Trot was desired by two witty peers,
To tell them the reason why asses have ears,
" 'A'nt please you," quoth John, "I'm not given to letters,
Nor dare I pretend to know more than my betters;
Howe'er, from this time I shall ne'er see your graces,
As I hope to be saved, without thinking of asses."

Oliver Goldsmith

EVERY MAN TO HIS OWN TRADE

An ass which saw a wolf running at him, while he was grazing in a meadow, pretended to be lame. When the wolf came up and asked what made him lame, he said that he had trodden on a thorn in jumping over a fence, and advised the wolf to pull it out before eating him, so that it would not prick its mouth. The wolf fell into the trap and lifted up the ass's foot. While it was intently examining the hoof the ass kicked it in the mouth and knocked out its teeth. "I have got what I deserved", said the wolf in this sorry plight. "My father taught me the trade of a butcher, and I had no business to meddle with doctoring".

Those who interfere with what does not concern them must expect to get into trouble.

Aesop's Fables
Translated by S. A. Handford

ONE MASTER AS GOOD AS ANOTHER

Poor men generally find that a change of government simply means exchanging one master for another – a truth which is illustrated in the following little anecdote.

A timid old man was grazing his donkey in a meadow when all of a sudden he was alarmed by the shouting of some enemy soldiers. "Run for it", he cried, "so that they can't catch us". But the donkey was in no hurry. "Tell me", said he: "if I fall into the conqueror's hands, do you think he will make me carry a double load?" "I shouldn't think so", was the old man's answer. – "Then what matter to me what master I serve, as long as I only have to bear my ordinary burden?"

Aesop's Fables
Translated by S. A. Handford

A GRIEVOUS LOSS

"And this," said he, putting the remains of a crust into his wallet, "and this should have been thy portion," said he, "hadst thou been alive to have shared it with me." I thought by the accent, it had been an apostrophe to his child; but 'twas to his ass, and to the very ass we had seen dead in the road, which had occasioned La Fleur's misadventure. The man seemed to lament it much; and it instantly brought into my mind Sancho's lamentation for his; but he did it with more true touches of nature.

The mourner was sitting upon a stone-bench at the door, with the ass's pannel and its bridle on one side, which he took up from time to time, then laid them down, look'd at them and shook his head. He then took his crust of bread out of his wallet again, as if to eat it; held it some time in his hand, then laid it upon the bit of his ass's bridle, looked wistfully at the little arrangement he had made, and then gave a sigh.

The simplicity of his grief drew numbers about him, and La Fleur amongst the rest, whilst the horses were getting ready; as I continued sitting in the post-chaise, I could see and hear over their heads.

He said he had come from Spain, where he had been from the furthest borders of Franconia; and he had got so far on his return home when his ass died. Everyone seemed desirous to know what business could have taken so old and poor a man so far a journey from his own home.

It had pleased Heaven, he said, to bless him with three sons, the finest lads in all Germany; but having in one week lost two of the eldest of them by the small-pox, and the youngest falling ill of the same distemper, he was afraid of being bereft of them all; and made a vow, if Heaven would not take him from him also, he would go in gratitude to St. Iago in Spain.

When the mourner got thus far on his story, he stopp'd to pay nature her tribute and wept bitterly.

He said, Heaven had accepted the conditions and that he had set out from his cottage with this poor creature, who had been a patient partner of his journey, that it had ate the same bread with him all the way and was unto him as a friend.

Everybody who stood about heard the poor fellow with concern. La Fleur offered him money. The mourner said he did not want it – it was not the value of the ass, but the loss of him. The ass, he said, he was assured loved him; and upon this told them a long story of a mischance upon their passage over the Pyrenean mountains, which had separated them from each other three days; during which time the ass had sought him as much as he had sought the ass, and that they had neither scarce eat or drank till they met.

Etching by George Stubbs A.R.A., 1724–1806

"Thou hast one comfort, friend," said I, "at least, in the loss of thy poor beast; I'm sure thou has been a merciful master to him." "Alas! said the mourner, I thought so, when he was alive, but now that he is dead I think otherwise. I fear the weight of myself and my afflictions together have been too much for him – they have shortened the poor creature's days and I fear I have them to answer for." "Shame on the world!" said I to myself; "did we love each other as this poor soul but loved his ass, 'twould be something."

Laurence Sterne
A Sentimental Journey Through France and Italy by Mr Yorick 1768

LOVE IN IDLENESS

On the First of April a certain Gentleman's Groom, Roger by Name, was walking his Master's Horses in some Fallow-Ground. There 'twas his good fortune to find a pretty Shepherdess, feeding her bleating Sheep, and harmless Lambkins, on the Brow of a neighbouring Mountain, in the Shade of an adjacent Grove: Near her, some frisking Kids tript it o'er a green Carpet of Nature's spreading; and to complete the Pastoral Landskip, There stood an Ass.

Roger, who was a Wag, had a dish of Chat with her; and after some If's, And's, and But's, Hem's, and Heigh's on her Side, got her in the mind to get up behind him, to go and see his Stable, and there take a Bit by the bye in a Civil way. While they were holding a Parley, the Horse directing his discourse to the Ass (for all Brute Beasts spoke that Year in divers Places) whisper'd these words in his Ear: Poor Ass, how I pity thee! Thou slavest like any Hack, I read it on thy Crupper; thou do'st well however, since God created thee to serve Mankind; thou art a very honest Ass; But not to be better Rub'd down, Curricomb'd, Trap'd, and Fed than thou art, seems to me indeed to be too hard a Lot. Alas! thou art all Rough-coated, in ill Plight; Jaded, Founder'd, Crestfallen, and Drooping like a Mooting Duck, and feedest there on nothing but coarse Grass, or Bryars and Thistles; Therefore do but Pace it along with me, and thou shalt see how we noble Steeds, made by Nature for War, are treated; come, thou'lt lose nothing by coming, I'll get thee a taste of my Fare. I 'troth, Sir, I can but love you and thank you, return'd the Ass; I'll wait on you, good Mr. Steed. Methink Gaffer Ass, you might as well have said, Sir Grandpaw Steed. Oh! Cry Mercy, good Sir Grandpaw, return'd the Ass; we Country Clowns are somewhat gross, and apt to knock Words out of joint; However, an't please you, I'll come after your Worship at some distance, lest for taking this Run, my Side should chance to be firk'd and curried with a vengeance, as 'tis but too often, the more's my sorrow.

The Shepherdess being got behind Roger, the Ass follow'd, fully Resolv'd to Bate like a Prince with Roger's Steed. But when they got to the Stable, the Groom who spy'd the grave Animal, order'd one of his Underlings to welcome him with the pitchfork, and curricomb him with a Cudgel. The Ass, who heard this, recommended himself mentally to the God Neptune, and was packing off, thinking, and syllogizing within himself thus; Had I not been an Ass, I had not come here among great Lords, when I must needs be sensible that I was only made for the Use of the small Vulgar: Aesop had given me fair Warning of this, in one of his Fables. Well, I must e'en scamper, or take what follows. With this he fell a Trotting, and Winsing, and Yerking, and Calcitrating, and Curveting and Bounding, and Springing, and Galloping full drive as if the Devil had been come for him *in propria persona*.

The Shepherdess, who saw the Ass scour off, told Roger that 'twas her Cattle, and desir'd he might be kindly us'd, or else she would not stir her foot over the Threshold. Friend Roger no sooner knew this, but he order'd him to be fetch'd in, and that my Master's Horses shou'd rather chop Straw for a Week together, than my Mistress's Beast should want his Belly-full of corn.

The most difficult point was to get him back; for in vain the Youngsters complimented and cox'd him to come; I dare not, said the Ass, I am bashful; and the more they strove by fair means to bring him with them the more the stubborn Thing was untoward, and flew out at heels; insomuch that they might have been there to this hour, had not his Mistress advis'd 'em to toss Oats in a Sieve or in a Blanket and call him; which was done, and made him wheel-about, and say, Oats with a witness, Oats shall go to pot, adveniat; Oats will do, there's evidence in the Case; but none of the Rubbing down, none of the Cudgelling. Thus melodiously singing, for as you know the Arcadian Bird's Note is very harmonious, he came to the Young Gentlemen of the Horse, alias Blackgarb, who brought him into the Stable.

When he was there, they plac'd him next to the great Horse, his Friend, Rubb'd him down, Curricomb'd him, laid clean Straw under him up to his Chin, and there he lay at Rack and Manger; the first stuff'd with sweet Hay, the latter with Oats; which when the Horse-Valets-de-Chambre sifted, he clapt down his Lugs to tell them by Signs that he would eat it but too well without sifting, and that he did not deserve so great an honour;

When they had well fed, quoth the Horse to the Ass, Well, poor Ass, how is it with thee now? How do'st thou like this fare? Thou wert so nice at first, a body had so much ado to get thee hither. By the Fig, answered the Ass, which one of our ancestors eating, Philemon died laughing, this is all sheer Ambrosia, good Sir Grandpaw. But what would you have an Ass say? Methinks all this is yet but half Cheer; Don't your Worships here use now and then to take a Leap? What Leaping do'st thou mean? ask'd the horse; the Devil leap thee, do'st thou take me for an Ass? I 'troth, Sir Grandpaw, quoth the Ass, I am somewhat a Blockhead, you know, and can't for the heart's blood of me learn so fast the Court-way of Speaking of you Gentlemen Horses; I mean, Don't you Stallionize it sometimes here among your metal'd Fillies? Tush, whispered the Horse, speak lower; for, by Bucephalus, if the Grooms but hear thee, they'll maul and belam me and thee thrice and three-fold; so that thou'lt have but little stomach to a Leaping bout. God so, Man, we dare not so much as grow stiff at the tip of the lowermost Snout, tho' 'twere but to leak or so, for fear of being Jirk'd and paid out of our Letchery. As for anything else, we are as happy as our Master, and perhaps more. By this Packsaddle, my old Acquaintance, quoth the Ass, I have done with you, a fart for thy Litter and Hay, and a fart for thy Oats; Give me the Thistles of our Fields, since there we leap when we list; Eat less, and Leap the more, I say; 'tis Meat, Drink and Cloth to us. Ah! Friend Grandpaw, it wou'd do thy heart good to see us at a Fair, when we hold our Provincial Chapter! Oh! how we Leap it while our Mistresses are selling their Goslins and other Poultry! With this they parted; Dixi: I have done.

François Rabelais
Pantagruel. Book V 1532–35

A PANACEA

A gentleman who died here today, told us of a trick his workmen played him this morning, which illustrates the superstition of the Irish.

He is repairing his house and sent a donkey and cart to fetch something in haste, which the builders stood in immediate need of. The time when it should have returned had elapsed, and Mr. L –, vexed at its non-arrival walked out on the road to see whether he could discover any appearance of the returning vehicle. At the foot of the hill was a smith's forge, round the door of which was assembled a crowd of persons. In the midst of these he descried his donkey standing stock-still, surrounded by a set of women, who were passing a miserable-looking half-naked child round and round over its back and under its body, while the empty cart was lying on the road side.

"What's all this foolery about?" exclaimaed Mr L –, making his way through the crowd, and not very well pleased to find that his errand had been stopped in the very outset.

"Oh! we're just done, yer honour – just this very minute – the donkey 'll be released now in less than no time."

"But," began Mr. L –, in no very complacent tone of remonstrance.

"Sure we're axing yer honour's pardon," said one of the women; "tis fits the weenoch has got, and we're curing him – passing him nine times nine under the donkey, yer honour."

"Don't you think," said Mr. L –, eyeing the starved and shivering infant, "if you were to get your child better clothed, with proper food and medicine, it would do him more good than all this nonsense?"

"Food, yer honour? – Och thin, if this don't cure him, troth and there's nothing else will."

Lady Chatterton
Rambles in the South of Ireland 1838–39

RARA AVIS

"Never . . . see . . . a dead postboy, did you?" inquired Sam . . . "No," rejoined Bob, "I never did." "No!" rejoined Sam triumphantly. "Nor never vill: and there's another thing no man never see, and that's a dead donkey, 'cept the gen'l'm'n in the black silk smalls as know'd the young 'ooman as kept a goat; and that was a French donkey, so wery likely he warn't wun o' the reglar breed."

Charles Dickens
Pickwick Papers 1837

WORDS TO THE WISE

If thou meet thine enemy's ox or his ass going astray, thou shalt surely bring it back to him again.

Exodus

'*The Cottage Children*', *engraving after Thomas Gainsborough, 1727–1788*

7. The Donkey Triumphant

THE DONKEY

When fishes flew and forests walked
And figs grew upon thorn,
Some moment when the moon was blood
Then surely I was born.

With monstrous head and sickening cry
And ears like errant wings,
The devil's walking parody
On all four-footed things.

The tattered outlaw of the earth,
Of ancient crooked will;
Starve, scourge, deride me: I am dumb,
I keep my secret still.

Fools! For I also had my hour;
One far fierce hour and sweet;
There was a shout about my ears,
And palms before my feet.

Gilbert Keith Chesterton *1900*

THE DONKEY OF GOD

One day as he [St. Francis] was walking among the ruins of monuments as old as the stone-age, he noticed he had gone farther than usual and was straying in a circle of queer structures that the natives called "Fairy Houses". He smiled as he thought of the fear the peasants had of these stone-chambers and the superstition that anyone resting within the circle would "dream true". He noticed a donkey standing in the shade of a stunted tree, but it did not appear in the least astonished to see him. Now that he observed it closer, he could not remember ever having seen a donkey so small. It was no larger than a large dog, a sheep-dog with unusually long ears. Its ankles were more delicate than a deer's and the eyes had a speaking softness. But the most peculiar feature was revealed to Francis only when he stood close. The colour was a soft pigeon-grey without a spot except for one distinguishing mark: a pattern made by two intersecting lines of black, one line running down the back from head to tail, the other line running across the shoulders. Presently, Francis noticed that the animal was speaking to him and he was aware that he understood it.

"Tell me, my good man," it was saying, "for I can see you are good, is there no justice in creation? Isn't it bad enough that we donkeys have to carry every sort of burden – twice as much as the much larger horse – without also being a joke among men and animals? Is that just? And if that were not enough, why should we be made still more foolish by having to wear such a disfiguring pattern on our back? Can you answer that?"

To his surprise, Francis heard himself replying to the little donkey as if he were a priest and it were one of his flock.

"Yes, my daughter, I think I can. There is a justice in all things, though we cannot see it at once. We must wait until the pattern is completed before we judge any of its parts. In your case the answer is easier than most, for you are the donkey of God".

"The donkey of God?" asked the little animal.

"Surely", replied Francis, amazed at the way he was talking, but keeping on in an even voice. "If you do not know your own story, I will tell it to you".

And Francis, who had never seen the creature before, and who certainly had never thought of its origin, heard himself telling this strange legend:

It was the morning of the Sixth Day. God had spent the First Day inventing Light. Then, seeing that continual light would be too cruel on the eyes, He made Darkness for relief. On the Second Day God had designed the seas and had put a clear border of sky about them to prevent the waters from overflowing. On the Third Day, being dissatisfied with the emptiness of a world of water, He had gathered the waters in one place and had put dry land carefully among the seas. He called the dry land Earth and liked it much better, especially after He had caused green things to grow and had planned fruit to come after the flower. He had told Himself it was good. On the Fourth Day God had looked at the widespread Heaven and realized it needed something. So he had put lights in it: a great gold light to rule the day, and a soft silver one to rule the night, and a lot of lesser lights to decorate the evening. And once more He had been pleased. On the Fifth Day He decided he wanted more motion and sound in the universe. So He had filled the waters with whales and minnows and the air with insects and eagles. He had smiled when the first whale, that island afloat, had blown his first spout, and His great heart had tightened when the lark, hoping to reach heaven, sang his first song.

And now it was the Sixth Day. The earth, God saw, needed life no less than the sea and sky. So early in the morning He began making animals. First He made small simple ones: the snake and the snail, the mouse and the mole, rat and rabbit, cat and dog, lamb and wolf, goat, mink, fox, hedge-hog, beaver, woodchuck and a hundred others, each after his kind. Then, watching them leap or crawl or dig or prowl, He tried the same design on an ever-growing scale. It was then He made donkey and deer, horse and cattle, lion and tiger, bear, buffalo, elk, the great apes, the giant lizards, the mammoths like mountains on the move. Then God, out of the humour of His heart, indulged himself in a few experiments. He made the giraffe with his feet in the mud, his long neck lost in the leaves, and his silly head trying to scrape the stars. He tied a bird and a snake together and made the ostrich, He took a lump of clay, shaped it, unshaped it, dug His thumb twice into it and threw it away – and that was the camel. He thought of a hillside with a tiny tail and nose-arm-fingers in one long trunk – and thus the elephant was made. He took some river-mud, breathed on it, changed His mind saying, "No animal that looked like that would want to live" – and it was the hippopotamus. When He saw these absurd shapes strut about, He laughed so long that the stars began to fall from their places – some of them are still so loose that they tremble in the sky – and, for a while, He did nothing at all.

But since He was God, He could not stop creating. So in the afternoon He looked at everything and said, "It is good". After a little while He added, "But it could be better. It lacks something".

All afternoon He sat pondering among the clouds. At last, toward evening, He said, "It is not enough like Me. I will take the very best soil from the earth, for this will be an earth-creature. I will mix it with water so he need not be afraid of the sea. I will knead it with air so he can trust himself in any element and even fly if he wishes. I will then put a spark of Myself deep in him so he may be God-like. And it will be Man."

When the animals heard this they began arguing with God. "Consider, O Lord", said the lion in his gentlest, most persuasive roar. He was already known as the king of beasts, so he spoke first. "Consider, O Lord, before You breathe life into the creature. If you make him of the elements, he will be master not only of them, but of us all".

"Yes", said the elephant with a gruff simplicity, "such an animal as Man will do no labour at all. He'll say he's not made for it, and we'll have to do his work for him."

"Not that we mind, Lord", hissed the serpent with false meekness. "But if you put your spark in him, he'll think he's divine. And after he's mastered us – not that *we* mind – he'll try to master what created him. And then –"

"And then," said God in the still small voice which was more terrible than thunder, "he will be part of Me again. Meanwhile, I have no need of advice from My own creations".

And so he made Man.

You are wondering, I see, what had become of the donkey. Up to now he had done nothing but listen and mind his own affairs. While the others were arguing with God or grumbling among themselves, the donkey calmly went on eating rose-leaves and lettuces and growing lovelier every minute. Perhaps I should have told you that he had been born the most perfect of four-footed creatures. He was very much like the donkeys of today except that his colour was softer, his eyes more tender, his ankles even more graceful – and, at that time, the long ears of his great-great-grandchildren did not disfigure his head. Instead of the grotesque flapping sails of the donkey of today, the original donkey had two of the finest, most perfectly shaped ears you can imagine. They were like those of a dainty fox, only smaller, and so wax-like that you could half see through them. Everything satisfied him; he feared nothing; the world was good. So he continued to munch lettuces and rose-leaves.

The donkey was so busy eating – it was at the beautiful beginning of things when there were no worms in the lettuces nor thorns on the roses – that he did not see God make the first man. Nor did he see Him, late in the night, creating the first woman. The next morning – it was Sunday – the other animals told him about it and said the man-animal was called Adam and the woman-animal was called Eve. A little tired of doing nothing but eating, the donkey joined the other beasts and peered into the garden where the two newest-born creatures were sitting. When he saw them he burst into the loudest and most ridiculous laugh on earth. It was like no sound that had ever been made; it was the first wild, weird, astonishing bray. Today only the smallest echoes are in the throat of all the donkeys, but then it rang so fiercely against the skies that it almost threw the fixed stars out of their courses.

"Ho-hee-haw!" screamed the donkey. "It is *too* funny! *Such* animals! They're made all wrong! No hide! No hoofs! Not even a tail! And so pink – so *naked*! God must have meant to put a coat of fleece on them and forgot it! Ho-hee-haw!"

Eve, frightened by the screaming and screeching, ran into the woods. Adam sprang to his feet.

"And look!" the donkey brayed in a still ruder laugh, while the other beasts roared and cackled and barked. "Look! The she-man runs on her hind legs! She doesn't even know how to walk! Ho-ho-hee-haw he-HAW!"

This was too much for Adam. He ran over to the donkey and grasped him by the ears. The donkey tried to pull himself free, but Adam held fast. As he tugged and Adam tightened, his ears began to stretch, grow long, longer. . . . And while they were pulling God suddenly appeared.

Said the Lord, "Because you have spoiled My day of rest and because you have made fun of My creation you shall be punished. Because you saw fit to laugh at your betters, you shall never cease from laughing. But no-one will listen with joy; your voice will be a mockery by day and a horror by night. The louder you laugh, the longer will you be despised. You shall serve man and be subject to him all the days of your life. Other animals shall serve him also: the horse, the cow, the elephant and the dog. But, unlike them, you shall work for man without winning his love. Unlike them, you shall resist him foolishly, and he shall beat you for it. You who are the most comely of My creatures shall be the most comic. Instead of roses you shall feed on thorns and thistles. You shall have a rope for a tail. And your ears shall remain long."

So it was decreed. And so it turned out. When Adam and Eve were forced to leave the Garden and go to work, the donkey went with them. Adam rode on the horse, the dog trotted at Eve's side, but it was the donkey who carried the tools, the spinning-wheel and all the household machinery. Throughout Adam's life the donkey was reminded of the saying about laughing last instead of first. Sometimes he was ashamed and dropped his long ears like a lop-eared rabbit; sometimes his pride came back and he refused to take another step. At such times Adam beat him and the donkey remembered the Lord's prophecy. He wondered how long the burdens would be piled upon him.

After Adam died the donkey thought things would go easier, but he soon realized his hardships were only beginning. He belonged, he discovered, not to one man but to all men. Cain, the brutal son of Adam, broke him to harness and made him drag a heavy plough. When Noah built the ark the donkey carried more timber than the elephant, but no one praised him for it. Forty days and forty nights the floating menagerie breasted the flood, and every day and most of the nights the other animals jeered and mocked him.

He knew now what it was to be laughed at. And when the windows of heaven were closed and the fountains of the flood went back into the heart of the sea, the donkey walked the earth again with meek eyes and bowed head. From that time on he swore to serve man faithfully and ask no reward.

At the building of Babel, the donkey was there, working willingly although he knew no tower built by hands would ever reach Heaven. After the city was deserted, the donkey helped Abraham with his flocks, and carried for Isaac, and wandered with Jacob. So, through Bible times, the donkey remained loyal to his masters. He brought Joseph and his twelve brothers together; he dragged bricks for the Hebrews during their long slavery in Egypt; he crossed the Red Sea with Moses; he was beaten for trying to save the wizard Balaam; he entered Canaan with Joshua.

He worked; he wandered; he did not die.

Years passed; centuries vanished. The donkey was in Palestine. His master was a carpenter in the little town of Nazareth, a good master by the name of Joseph, though far different from the Joseph who had become a ruler in the land of Egypt. He had worked for him a long time, and he had served his owner well. A few years ago, when Joseph and his wife Mary were on their wanderings, the little donkey carried them everywhere without complaining. They were terribly poor and innkeepers had no room for them. The donkey trudged on, carrying his load that seemed to grow heavier with each step. For a long day and a longer night, he plodded toward the distant haven, never stopping or stumbling till he brought them to the little town of Bethlehem. That night, in a cattle stall, Mary's child had been born.

The donkey obeyed his master, but he worshipped his master's small son. The child was not only beautiful, but even as perfect as he seemed to his mother. Goodness shone from his eyes; miracles, they said, flowed from his hands. The donkey believed it, for he had seen one performed.

Once, when playing with some other children in the streets of Nazareth, the carpenter's son picked up some clay from the gutter and kneaded it into a shape. His companions gathered around to watch him.

"Good", said Simon, "let's all do it. What shall we model?"

"Let's make horses", cried Zadok, the son of the priest. "When I grow up I'm going to have six horses of my own – two white ones, two black ones and two horses with many-coloured coats".

"Stupid!" said Azor, the broom-maker's child. "There are no horses with many-coloured coats. Besides, horses are too hard to model. Let's make pigeons".

So they started to make pigeons of the clay. After a while Zadok called out, "I've made seven. How many have the rest of you?"

"Five," said Zithri, the beggar's boy.

"Four," said Simon.

"Three," said Azor.

"Two," said Jesus, who was the carpenter's son.

"Only two!" sneered Zadok. "And not even good ones. Mine look much more like pigeons than yours!"

"You are right," said Jesus and he tossed his aside. But though the clay pigeons were thrown, they did not fall to the ground. Instead, they hung in the air, spread wings and flew away.

The other children stared for a moment and then grew angry. "He's playing tricks on us!" cried Zadok, son of the priest. "Let's play a trick on him!" The others joined Zadok and soon they had tied the little Jesus tightly. The cord bit deep into his wrists but he did not cry.

"He's just making believe he's brave," said Zadok. "He acts as if he were a king".

"All right," jeered Azor. "Let him be king".

"I'll get him a crown," shouted Zithri.

They pulled down part of a withered rose-tree and twisted two small branches into a crown. They pressed this upon his forehead and cried, "King Jesus! Hail to King Jesus!" Then they ran away laughing, while tears stood in the eyes of the carpenter's son.

The donkey had seen it all, had seen that the hands of Jesus were still tied and that the child could not remove the crown of thorns. Then he nuzzled his soft nose along the child's shoulder, raised his head and, though the thorns stabbed his lips, lifted the piercing weight from Jesus' forehead. He tugged at the cords till he freed the child's hands; then he carried him home.

More years passed. Jesus had gone away. Though the donkey did not know it, the carpenter's son had grown from childhood to manhood, had travelled and studied, had healed the sick, restored eyesight to the blind, cast out devils, had suffered untold hardships. But now the moment had come; Jesus was to enter Jerusalem in triumph.

It was a tremendous moment; one that must be celebrated in the proper manner. Naturally, Jesus could not enter the queen-city of Palestine on foot; he must ride, they said, on a charger worthy of the event. So the Archangel Michael called all the animals before Jesus that they might plead their case.

"Choose me," said the lion. "I am king of the beasts; you are a king among men. Men respect royalty – but only when they recognize it! When the people of Jerusalem see you riding on my back, they will know you are of noble blood and they will bow down and fear you. With me as your mascot, they will never dare oppose, but follow you in terror".

"Choose me," said the eagle. "I am lord of the upper air. Choose me and you will have power to leave the earth and fly on the very back of the wind. I will take you to the borders of the sky there, from heights unknown to man, you shall see everything that happens below. When you enter Jerusalem flying between my strong wings, the people will believe you are a god and they will worship."

"Choose me," said the mole. "I go where the eagle is helpless and the lion cannot follow. Choose me and I will give you the keys of earth. I will guide you to the roots of power, to secrets buried beneath the stones. I know where every vein of gold is hidden; my home is among the caves of rubies, hills of emerald, ledges of pure diamond. Choose me and you will be greater than the greatest; you will be able to buy empires; you will not only be a king, but King of kings".

"The great ones laugh at the treasures", whispered the fox. "Who but a fool desires gold and glittering pebbles that turn men against each other with greed and jealousy? Choose me and I will give you cunning. I will show you how to outwit all men and overcome your enemies with shrewdness. Choose me and I will teach you cleverness that is better than wealth and craft that is stronger than strength".

"Craft!" trumpeted the elephant. "Craft and cunning are for knaves who will never be wise. Choose me and I will give you true wisdom. I am the oldest of living creatures; my years span a century and I have watched the comings and goings of all the races. Choose me and you will rule the changing mind of the unchanging world".

"Choose me," lowed the cow. "I am sacred, India and Egypt worship me. I feed the world",

"Choose me," bellowed the dragon. "I will spread fire before you and magic wherever you go".

"Choose me!" neighed the horse. "I am swift as rage. The glory of my nostrils is terrible to the enemy. I swallow the ground; I laugh at fear".

"Choose me!" screamed the camel. "Choose me! Choose Me!" cried all the animals separately and in chorus. Only the donkey was silent.

"And what can you give?" asked Jesus, speaking for the first time and turning to the dusty little fellow. "What have you to promise?"

"Nothing," murmured the donkey. "Nothing. I am the lowest of all God's creatures and the least."

But Jesus remembered. "The lowest shall be lifted up", he said, "and the last shall be first".

And so the meekest of men chose the meekest of animals. And they entered Jerusalem together.

But the great moment passed. Proud Jerusalem jeered at the carpenter's son even as it had stoned the prophets before him, and only a handful of poor folk listened to his words. He was despised and rejected. The people turned against him. He was imprisoned on a false charge and condemned to death. They put a crown of thorns upon his head and made him carry his own cross.

It was while Jesus was struggling up the hill that the donkey saw him for the last time. Their sad eyes met.

"No," said Jesus. "You cannot help me now. Yet, since you have done more for me than have most men, you shall be rewarded. I cannot undo what God has done; what He has ordained must be carried out. But I can soften his decree. True, you will have to fetch and carry and feed on thorns. Yet these things will never again be hard for you. Because you carried me three times, so shall you be able to carry three times as much as animals thrice your size – and your load will seem lighter than theirs. You suffered thorns for my sake; so shall you be nourished when others can find nothing to feed on. You shall eat the thorns and nettles of the field – and they shall taste like sweet salads. You bore me when I grew to manhood, when I was a child, and even my mother before I was born. So shall you bear my cross – but you shall bear it without pain. Here –!" And as Jesus touched the shoulders of the donkey, a velvet-black cross appeared on the back of the kneeling animal.

And Jesus, shouldering his burden, climbed up Calvary . . .

Francis heard the last syllable leave his lips in a kind of wonder. His tiredness had gone: everything in him was full of strength. He was surprised to see that the sun had set and that a little horned moon had come into the sky one horn pointing to Assisi. He thought he understood the sign. When he turned back, the donkey had disappeared. The field was dark. But a light greater than the moon's was on Francis' face.

Louis Untermeyer
From: *Reminiscences of Affection,*
by Victor Gollancz 1932

BALAAM'S ASS

And Balaam rose up in the morning and saddled his ass and went with the princes of Moab.

And God's anger was kindled because he went: and the angel of the Lord stood in the way for an adversary against him. Now he was riding upon his ass and his two servants were with him.

And the ass saw the angel of the Lord standing in the way and his sword drawn in his hand: and the ass turned aside out of the way and went into the field: and Balaam smote the ass to turn her into the way.

But the angel of the Lord stood in a path of the vineyards, a wall being on this side and a wall on that side.

And when the ass saw the angel of the Lord, she thrust herself unto the wall and crushed Balaam's foot against the wall: and he smote her again.

And the angel of the Lord went further and stood in a narrow place where was no way to turn either to the right hand or to the left.

And when the ass saw the angel of the Lord, she fell down under Balaam: and Balaam's anger was kindled and he smote the ass with a staff.

And the Lord opened the mouth of the ass and she said unto Balaam, What have I done unto thee that thou hast smitten me these three times?

And Balaam said unto the ass, Because thou hast mocked me: I would there were a sword in mine hand, for now would I kill thee.

And the ass said unto Balaam, am not I thine ass upon which thou hast ridden ever since I was thine unto this day? Was I ever wont to do so unto thee? And he said, Nay.

Then the Lord opened the eyes of Balaam, and he saw the angel of the Lord standing in the way and his sword drawn in his hand: and he bowed down his head and fell flat on his face.

And the angel of the Lord said unto him, Wherefore hast thou smitten thine ass these three times? Behold, I went out to withstand thee, because thy way is perverse before me.

And the ass saw me and turned from me these three times: unless she had turned from me, surely now also I had slain thee and saved her alive.

And Balaam said unto the angel of the Lord, I have sinned: for I knew not that thou stoodest in the way against me: now therefore, if it displease thee, I will get me back again.

And the angel of the Lord said unto Balaam, Go with the men: but only the word I shall speak unto thee, that thou shalt speak. So Balaam went with the princes of Balak.

The Fourth Book of Moses, called Numbers

Who hath sent out the wild ass free? or who hath loosed the bands of the wild ass?

Whose house I have made the wilderness, and the barren land his dwellings.

He scorneth the multitude of the city, neither regardeth he the crying of the driver.

The range of the mountains is his pasture, and he searcheth after every green thing.

Book of Job

DONKEYS AT CORFU

Always the donkeys, laden with sticks for kindling,
With olives, bottles of wine, charcoal and sacks of flour,
Green-stuff piled on thin rumps,
Wooden saddles chafing bony backs,
Panniers waggling smothered in miniature forests of ferns, bracken, pine-cones,
Branches of cypress and juniper.

Or topped by an old man, wrinkled as his own olives,
An old woman, black-dressed, white-coiffed,
Spinning from her distaff as she rides.
Sometimes the children follow, black-eyed and merry,
Laughing, teasing, prodding the poor beasts,
The thin, grey, starved, indomitable donkeys.

In Corfu town horses wear tinselled bonnets,
Flowers and gay necklaces of blue and yellow beads
Against worry or the evil eye,
Yet why should a town-horse worry?
What should a town-horse fear?
Even the proud cock of Pelekas sports an amber necklace
Gleaming through its golden feathers.
But never the donkeys;
Burdened and overworked, they may neither fear nor worry.

When the incredible stillness of the night
Is broken by an ass braying,
Perhaps they are lamenting the sleepless hardship of their lives;
Perhaps to some St. Francis praying?

Joan Warburg *1968*

THE PRAYER OF THE DONKEY

O God who made me
to trudge along the road,
always
to carry heavy loads always
and to be beaten
always,
give me great courage and gentleness.
One day let somebody understand me –
that I may no longer want to weep
because I can never say what I mean
and they make fun of me.
Let me find a juicy thistle
and make them give me time to pick it,
And Lord, one day let me find again
my little brother of the Christmas crib.

Amen

Translated from the French of Carmen Bernos de Gasztold by Rumer Godden

FESTIVAL OF FOOLS

Amongst the buffooneries of the Festival of Fools one of the most remarkable was the introduction of an ass into the church, where various pranks were played with the animal. At Autun the ass was led with great ceremony to the church under a cloth of gold, the corners of which were held by four canons; and on entering the sacred edifice the animal was wrapt in a rich cope, while a parody of the mass was performed. A regular Latin liturgy in glorification of the ass was chanted on these occasions, and the celebrant priest imitated the braying of the ass. At Beauvais the ceremony was performed every year on the fourteenth of January. A young girl with a child in her arms rode on the back of the ass in imitation of the Flight into Egypt. Escorted by the clergy and the people she was led in triumph from the cathedral to the parish church of St. Stephen. There she and her ass were introduced into the chancel and stationed on the left side of the altar; and a long mass was performed which consisted of scraps borrowed indiscriminately from the services of many church festivals throughout the year. In the intervals the singers quenched their thirst: the congregation imitated their example; and the ass was fed and watered. The services over, the animal was brought from the chancel into the nave, where the whole congregation, clergy and laity mixed up together, danced round the animal and brayed, like asses.

Sir James Frazer *The Golden Bough 1890*

'The Flight into Egypt' by Gaudenzio Ferrari c. 1480–1546

HYMN OF THE ASS

From Eastern climes
Came the ass,
Beautiful and most strong,
Excellently adapted for burdens.
    Hey, Sir Ass, come and sing,
    Show you teeth well,
    You shall have lots of hay
    And oats in plenty.

Lazy were his steps
If the stick were lacking,
And the goad ceased
To prick him in the rear.

Gold from Arabia,
Frankincense and myrrh from Saba,
Brings into the Church
The strength of the ass.

When he draws carts
With a heavy load
His jaw champs
The hard fodder.

Behold the son of the yoke
With great ears,
The excellent ass,
Lord of asses.

In leaping he overcomes mules,
Deer and the chamois;
Swift above dromedaries
Of Madian.

He devours barley with its ears,
And the thistle;
Wheat from the chaff
He separates on the threshing-floor.

Say Amen, O Ass,
Now full of grass,
Amen, Amen repeat;
You despise what is old.
Hey, Go
Lovely Sir Ass, go away!
Fine mouth, sing away!

Phosphor Mallam
Translation of *The Prose of the Ass*,
sung in church at the mediaeval Feasts of Fools

HOSANNA IN THE HIGHEST

And when they drew nigh unto Jerusalem, and were come to Bethphage, unto the mount of Olives, then sent Jesus two disciples,

Saying unto them, Go into the village over against you, and straightway ye shall find an ass tied, and a colt with her: loose them, and bring them unto me.

And if any man say ought unto you, ye shall say, The Lord hath need of them; and straightway he will send them.

All this was done, that it might be fulfilled which was spoken by the prophet, saying

Tell ye the daughter of Sion, Behold, thy King cometh unto thee, meek, and sitting upon an ass, and a colt the foal of an ass.

And the disciples went, and did as Jesus commanded them,

And brought the ass, and the colt, and put on them their clothes, and they set him thereon.

And a very great multitude spread their garments in the way; others cut down branches from the trees, and strawed them in the way.

And the multitudes that went before, and that followed, cried, saying, Hosanna to the Son of David: Blessed is he that cometh in the name of the Lord; Hosanna in the highest.

And when he was come into Jerusalem, all the city was moved, saying, who is this?

And the multitude said, This is Jesus the prophet of Nazareth of Galilee.

St. Matthew

'Christ on an Ass'
by an anonymous Polish artist, c.1470

TRIPTYCH

The dashing 'chaser, head on high,
Told of his triumphs – "There was I,
Baulked at the Brook, but in the straight,
I showed 'em how to carry weight!"

The war horse rolled a fiery eye,
Dreaming of battles – "There was I,
The equine tank . . . Ah, Chivalry,
The very name revolves round me".

The pony, tossing tangled hair,
Neighed "Ere they bred you, I was there!
When man chased mammoths 'neath the sky,
And painted caverns – there was I".

The donkey pricked his patient ears
As memories drifted down the years . . .
Then spoke: "I heard a child's first cry,
And by His manger, there was I".

Joan Wanklyn *1968*

THE MAN WITH THE DONKEY

This is the story of an ordinary man who did extraordinary things in a critical situation. He was a plain private – a stretcher-bearer on Gallipoli. On the day after the landing he found a wandering donkey feeding idly in a gulley. He was one of the few men who knew how to handle donkeys, for he had loved them from his childhood. The idea seized his mind that this donkey would be useful to carry men with leg wounds from forward positions to the casualty station on the Beach.

Once he got going there was no stopping him. "The Man With The Donkey" became one of the familiar sights of Anzac. Day after day and into the nights he carried an amazing number of wounded men down the shrapnel-swept valley and saved innumerable lives at the risk, and finally at the cost, of his own.

He never suspected that he was a hero; he did what seemed to him the obvious thing to do, completely free of any self-consciousness.

Simpson became the glowing symbol of the courage and service of the stretcher-bearers. On the day of the Landing he carried with the other bearers, but was reported missing from his unit on the second day. Having carried two heavy men in succession down the awful slopes of Shrapnel Gully and through the Valley of Death he annexed a donkey that he found nibbling in one of the gullies. It responded to the sure touch of the friendly man with the experience he had gained as a boy in far-away summer holidays on the South Shields sands and probably welcomed his company after the terrors of the Landing and the pandemonium that followed. They were a quaint pair and from that day they were inseparable.

So he began to work as a lone unit and his Colonel, recognizing the value of his service, allowed him to continue and required him to report only once a day at the Field Ambulance.

His daily trip was up Shrapnel Gully and into Monash Gully and the deadly zone around Quinn's Post. He brought out the men to where he had left his donkey under cover and took them to the dressing station on the Beach. Fearless for himself, he was always considerate for his donkey. On the return journeys he carried water for the wounded.

He called the donkey by a variety of names according to his mood. Sometimes it was "Abdul", mostly "Duffy", occasionally "Murphy" – reminiscent of Murphy's Circus at South Shields. Brigadier-General C. H. Jess remembered one night when he heard a quick patter of feet outside his dugout and the cheerful voice of Simpson calling "Come on, Queen Elizabeth" – calling his donkey after the great battleship.

He himself was variously called Scotty, Murphy, Simmie and generally

"The Man With The Donk"....

E. C. Buley tells how, when the enfilading fire down the valley was at its worst and orders were posted that the ambulance men must not go out, the Man and the Donkey continued placidly at their work. At times they held trenches of hundreds of men spell-bound, just to see them at their work. Their quarry lay motionless in an open patch, in easy range of a dozen Turkish rifles. Patiently the little donkey waited under cover, while the man crawled through the thick scrub until he got within striking distance. Then a lightning dash, and he had the wounded man on his back and was making for cover again. In those fierce seconds he always seemed to bear a charmed life.

Once in cover he tended his charge with quick, skilful movements. "He had hands like a woman's", said one who thinks he owes his life to the man and the donkey. Then the limp form was balanced across the back of the patient animal, and, with a slap on its back and the Arab donkey-boy's cry for "Gee", the man started off for the beach, the donkey trotting unruffled by his side.

Most of his casualties were wounded in the legs and so could not walk to the clearing-station. Sometimes he was seen holding an unconscious man with one arm and guiding the donkey with the other, and having handed him over to the Medical staff he returned for more....

F. W. Dyke, one of the Gallipoli originals, told me of a rare occasion when his donkey was proving obstinate. A Padre was standing by waiting to accompany Simpson, but with all his coaxing the donkey wouldn't move. At last Simpson turned to the Padre and said, "Padre, this old donkey has been tied up with some mules and has acquired some of their mulish habits. Would you move along the beach a little way, as I'll have to speak to him in Hindustani, and, Padre, I wouldn't like you to think I was swearing at him".

He camped with his donkey at the Indian Mountain Battery Mule Camp and seemed very much at home with them. But he slept little and begrudged time to eat. The Indians had their own name for him – "Bahadur" which, being interpreted, means "the bravest of the brave"....

In the middle of May, the Turks made their most violent attempt to drive the Anzacs from the cliffs and throw them into the sea.

Morning came, the sun rose behind the teeming hosts, machine-guns and rifles mowed them down in rows and piled them into barriers. Still they came on, rushing wildly at the sandbag lines, scrambling over them, only to die at the ends of rifles which scorched their skins.

The conflict raged on until nearly eleven o'clock in the morning. The great assault had finished and failed. No trench was taken.

It was on the final fling of the attack on the morning of the 19th that Simpson made his last journey with his donkey up the Gully.

That morning Simpson went up the valley to the water-guard where he usually had breakfast, but it was not ready so he went on his way. "Never mind", he called cheerily to the cook, "get me a good dinner when I come back".

On the way down he was shot through the heart by a machine-gun bullet at the very spot where General Bridges was killed on the 15th. Andy Davidson and others who were carrying him from the top of the Gully had just spoken to him as they were going up. When Simpson fell beside the donkey, Davidson says: "We went back and covered his body and put it in a dugout by the side of the track and carried on with our job. We went back for him about 6.30 p.m. and he was buried at Hell Spit on the same evening". They made a simple wooden cross and set it on his grave with the name "John Simpson" – nothing else. One of the First Battalion missed him from the Gully that day and asked "Where's Murphy?" "Murphy's at Heaven's gate" answered the Sergeant, "helping the soldiers through".

What became of the little donkey with the long ears and the sturdy grey back that was so often stained red? Dale Collins and Dr. Bean support the oft-repeated statement that he became the pet of the 6th Mountain Battery Indians, who took him with them at the evacuation. So perhaps he lived out his years contentedly munching green grass on the peaceful plains of India with far-away recurring memories of that strange man who adopted him in his loneliness and with whom he walked the long rough trail up and down Shrapnel Gully.

One day Philadelphia Robertson contemplated the bronze statuette of Simpson and his Donkey beside the Shrine of Remembrance which dominates Melbourne's St. Kilda Road and looks out over Port Philip Bay which Simpson knew well, and she went home to write this poem:

Would it seem strange to you
If somewhere in Elysian fields
Cropping the herbage by a crystal stream,
Wandered the little ass, tall Simpson's friend?
Or strange at all,
If, down the hill, beneath the flowering trees,
By meadows starred with lilac and with rose,
Came Simpson, singing, his brown hands
With celestial carrots filled
For his old friend?
To me, not strange at all,
Amidst the beauty of some shining sphere
They surely move –
Those deathless hosts of Christlike chivalry.

Sir Irving Benson
The Man With The Donkey,
John Simpson Kirkpatrick 1964

PRAYER TO GO TO PARADISE WITH THE DONKEY

When it behoves me to go to you, O my God, let
it be upon a day when the country for a fête
powders the road. I want, as I did here below,
to choose a way to go, just as I like to go,
to Paradise, where are in full daylight the clear stars.
I'll take my walking stick, and on the highroad's rise
I'll go, and I'll say to the donkeys: my friends!
I am Francis Jammes, and I am going to Paradise,
for there is not a hell in the land of the good God;
I shall tell them: Come, sweet friends of the blue sky, who with a nod,
poor, loved beasts, with a quick movement of the ear, chase away
the flat, tormenting flies, the buffets, and the bees. . . .

O let me come before you in the middle of these beasts
that I love so because they lower their heads, indeed
very gently and stop still, joining their little feet
in a most piteous way, very kindly, that brings tears.
I shall arrive followed by their thousands of ears,
followed by those who carried baskets on their flanks,
by those drawing clownwise their somersaulting carts
or cartloads of feathery dusters and tins,
by those back clattered with dented water-cans,
by she-asses as wide as leathern bottles, halting often,
by those one dresses up in little pantaloons
because of the wet sores, blue and aching, make
infatuated flies that surround them in rings.

My God, make it be that with these donkeys I come to you.
Make it be that angels lead us forward in peace
to tufted river-banks where tremble bright cherries
sleek and glossy as the laughing flesh of young girls,
and make it be that leaning, in this place of souls' ease
over your divine waters, I shall be like the donkeys
that will watch their humble and sweet poverty move
towards the limpidity of eternal love.

Vernon Watkins
Translated from the French of Francis Jammes

ENVOI

THE ASS

The long-drawn bray of the ass
In the Sicilian twilight –

All mares are dead!
All mares are dead!
Oh-h!
Oh-h-h!
Oh-h-h-h-h-h!!
I can't bear it, I can't bear it.
I can't!
Oh, I can't!
Oh –
There's one left!
There's one left!
One!
There's one . . . left. . . .

So ending on a grunt of agonized relief.
This is the authentic Arabic interpretation of the braying of the ass.
And Arabs should know.

And yet, as his brass-resonant howling yell resounds through the Sicilian twilight
I am not sure –

His big furry head,
His big, regretful eyes,
His diminished, drooping hindquarters,
His small toes.

Such a dear!
Such an ass!
With such a knot inside him!

He regrets something that he remembers.
That's obvious.

The Steppes of Tartary,
And the wind in his teeth for a bit,
And *noli me tangere.*

Ah then, when he tore the wind with his teeth,
And trod the wolves underfoot,
And over-rode his mares as if he were savagely leaping an obstacle, to set his teeth in the sun . . .

Somehow, alas, he fell in love,
And was sold into slavery.

He fell into the rut of love,
Poor ass, like man, always in rut,
The pair of them alike in that.

All his soul in his gallant member
And his head gone heavy with the knowledge of desire
And humiliation.

The ass was the first of all animals to fall finally into love,
From obstacle-leaping pride,
Mare obstacle,
Into love, mare-goal, and the knowledge of love.

Hence Jesus rode him in the Triumphant Entry.
Hence his beautiful eyes.
Hence his ponderous head, brooding over desire, and downfall, Jesus, and a pack-saddle,
Hence he uncovers his big ass-teeth and howls in that agony that is half insatiable desire and half unquenchable humiliation.
Hence the black cross on his shoulders.

The Arabs were only half right, though they hinted the whole;
Everlasting lament in everlasting desire.

See him standing with his head down, near the Porta Cappuccini,
Asinello, Ciuco,
Somaro;
With the half-veiled, beautiful eyes, and the pensive face not asleep,
Motionless, like a bit of rock.

Has he seen the Gorgon's head, and turned to stone?
Alas, Love did it.
Now he's a jackass, a pack-ass, a donkey, somaro, burro, with a boss piling loads on his back.
Tied by the nose at the Porta Cappuccini.
And tied in a knot, inside, dead-locked between two desires:

To overleap like a male all mares as obstacles
In a leap at the sun;
And to leap in one last heart-bursting leap like a male at the goal of a mare.
And there end.
Well, you can't have it both roads.

Hee! Hee! Ehee! Ehow! Ehaw!! Oh! Oh! Oh-h-h!
The wave of agony bursts in the stone that he was,
Bares his long ass's teeth, flattens his long ass's ears, straightens his donkey neck,
And howls his pandemonium on the indignant air.

Yes, it's a quandary.
Jesus rode on him the first burden on the first beast of burden.
Love on a submissive ass.
So the tale began.

But the ass never forgets.
The horse, being nothing but a nag, will forget.
And men, being mostly geldings and knacker-boned hacks, have almost all forgot.
But the ass is a primal creature, and never forgets.

The Steppes of Tartary,
And Jesus on a meek ass-colt: mares: Mary escaping to Egypt: Joseph's cudgel.

Hee! Hee! Ehee! Ehow-ow!-ow! – aw! – aw! – aw!
All mares are dead!

Or else I am dead!
One of us, or the pair of us,
I don't know-ow! – ow!
Which!
Not sure-ure-ure
Quite which!
Which!

D. H. Lawrence
Birds, Beasts and Flowers 1923

INDEX